AIN'T I A WOMAN!

A Book of Women's Poetry from Around the World

AIN'T I A WOMAN!

A Book of Women's Poetry from Around the World

Edited by
Illona Linthwaite

WINGS BOOKS
NEW YORK • AVENEL, NEW JERSEY

FOR
Peter and Jack,
Peter L, Jane, Cadence, Katherine, Annabelle,
and for the women who worked so hard to bring
AIN'T I A WOMAN! to the stage:
Marcia, Cordelia, Penny, Gail, Carol, Charmaine

This 1993 edition is published by Wings Books,
distributed by Outlet Book Company, Inc.,
a Random House Company, 40 Engelhard Avenue,
Avenel, New Jersey 07001, by arrangement
with Peter Bedrick Books.

Random House
New York • Toronto • London • Sydney • Auckland

Published in 1990 by PETER BEDRICK BOOKS
2112 Broadway, New York, NY 10023
Published by agreement with Virago Press Ltd, London

Printed and bound in the United States of America

Library of Congress Cataloging-in-Publication Data
Ain't I a woman! : a book of women's poetry from
    around the world / edited by Illona Linthwaite.
            p.   cm.
        ISBN 0-517-09365-0
        1. Poetry—Women authors.   2. Women—Poetry.
    I. Linthwaite, Illona, 1945-
    PN6109.9.A36   1993
    808.81'9352042—dc20   93-13201
                                       CIP

8 7 6 5 4 3 2 1

Ain't I A Woman! has its beginnings in 1983, when Illona Linthwaite began gathering the poems for a theatrical performance which toured Britain. On stage it took the form of a direct exchange between a black and a white woman, the voices speaking to each other across the centuries. Now, in extended book form, the collection affirms both the differences and the common ground between women, pursuing themes of love, injustice, motherhood and loss, and the oppressions of race and class. In their myriad ways, the 150 poems are a triumphant assertion of Sojourner Truth's famous challenge: 'Ain't I A Woman'.

Illona Linthwaite was born in Wiltshire in 1945. Since training at the Rose Bruford School of Speech and Drama, she has worked for many years in the theatre as an actor and teacher, appearing throughout Britain and Europe with such companies as the National Theatre and the Royal Shakespeare Company. She now lives in London.

Here is no sacrificial I,
Here are more I's than yet were in one human,
Here I reveal our common mystery:
I give you woman.

Anna Wickham

CONTENTS

vii

ACKNOWLEDGEMENTS

Permission to reproduce the following poems is gratefully acknowledged: Dazzly Anderson for 'Some Men', copyright © Dazzly Anderson 1987; Maya Angelou and Random House Inc. for 'On Ageing' from *And Still I Rise*, copyright © 1978 by Maya Angelou; Maya Angelou and Hirt Music Inc., c/o Gerald Purcell Associates Ltd. for 'They Went Home' from *Just Give Me a Cool Drink of Water 'Fore I Diiie*, copyright © by Hirt Music Inc. 1969; Pat Arrowsmith and Virago Press Ltd for 'Political Activist Living Alone' from *Bread and Roses*, copyright © Pat Arrowsmith 1982; Pat Arrowsmith for 'The Day I Once Dreamed' from *Thin Ice* (Greater London Region CND), copyright © Pat Arrowsmith 1982; Astra and Virago Press Ltd for 'now or never' from *Bread and Roses*, copyright © Astra 1973; 'A Women's Issue' reprinted by permission of Margaret Atwood, from *True Stories*, Oxford University Press 1981, copyright © 1981 Margaret Atwood; Josephine Balmer and Brilliance Books for her translations of three poems by Sappho beginning 'Lucky bridegroom', 'already old age' and 'Immortal Aphrodite' from *Sappho: Poems and Fragments*, copyright © Josephine Balmer 1984; Himani Bannerji for 'Paki Go Home', from *Canadian Women Poets*, a feminist quarterly (Fireweed Publishers), copyright © Himani Bannerji 1986; Willis Barnstone and Schocken Books Inc. for translations of 'After he stripped off my clothes' by Villana, 'My husband is the same man' by Sila, 'A free woman' by Sumangala and 'I see a man who is dull' (anon.) reprinted by permission of Schocken Books Inc. from *A Book of Women Poets from Antiquity to Now* edited by Aliki Barnstone and Willis Barnstone, copyright © Schocken Books Inc. 1980; Valerie Bloom and Bogle-L'Ouverture for 'Wha Fe Call I' from *Touch Mi, Tell Mi*, copyright © Valerie Bloom 1983; Geoffrey Bownas, Anthony Thwaite and Penguin Books Ltd for their translation of 'Sent from the capital to her elder daughter' by Lady Otomo of Sakanoe, from *The Penguin Book of Japanese Verse* translated and introduced by Geoffrey Bownas and Anthony Thwaite, copyright © Geoffrey Bownas and Anthony Thwaite 1964. Reproduced by Penguin Books Ltd, p. 60; Gwendolyn Brooks for 'The Bean Eaters' from *Selected Poems* copyright © Gwendolyn Brooks 1959; Maureen Burge and Virago Press Ltd for 'Disillusion' and 'The Diet' from *Bread and Roses*, copyright © Maureen Burge; Dinah Butler for 'Do You Fancy Me?', 'One Life', 'to my father', copyright © Dinah Butler 1985; Nurunnessa Choudhury for 'The Sun Witness', 'Blue Specks', 'Death of a Dove', 'I See Cleopatra' from *I See Cleopatra and Other Poems*, Basement Publishing Project; Nadia Christen-

PREFACE

Ain't I A Woman began its life in the theatre. Like many performers before me, I had wanted to create my own show. My involvement with poetry had started much earlier and I had always been interested in its dramatic potential. Ideas gathered as I read women's poetry more widely than I had ever done before. Originally, I had intended that the show be performed on my own, but thoughts of a dialogue were beginning to emerge. I began to look for another actress and it was at this time that I had the good fortune to meet Marcia Tucker. I asked her if she was interested in creating a show with me – she was. We worked together for a while before deciding that a third eye was necessary and then asked Cordelia Monsey to direct us.

The process of choosing, eliminating and placing the poems was exhilarating and sometimes painful, but slowly we wove the voices of many women, past and present into a dramatic exchange. I am indebted to Marcia and Cordelia for the love, commitment and sheer hard work they put into the show – it was very much a combined effort and the results were extraordinary for all of us. My deep thanks also to Charmaine Crowell with whom I performed the show in America.

It had been quite clear to us that no poem should be included simply because it provided a useful link or stopgap. Each poem had to be there in its own right. The same is true of the book. Every poem has its own particular voice and truth. There is a heightened sense of drama too, I feel, if one can move through time and half way round the world in the space of a page.

The original content has quadrupled and the concepts broadened. I have tried to capture the same flavour in the book that we discovered in the show, although the earlier structure has completely disappeared. The poems move more directly from youth to old age, mainly because links that are obvious in the theatre can seem tenuous, even non-existent, on the page. The first two poems are exceptions: 'The House of Desire' (1st Part) by Sherley Anne Williams and 'Warning' by Jenny Joseph – these are poems which stayed with me constantly. They opened the play and it seems entirely appropriate that they should introduce the book. The title *Ain't I A Woman* is taken from abolitionist Sojourner Truth's famous speech made at the Women's Rights Convention at Akron, Ohio in 1852, which Erlene Stetson has adapted to poetry.

The poems in this anthology mean many different things to me and I should like to end with a thought from one of them:

We need
A kind of acceptance
Short of blind
That to our limits
There be sent
The mercy of astonishment.

Illona Linthwaite, May 1987

xvii

AIN'T I A WOMAN!

A Book of Women's Poetry from Around the World

▮▮ SHERLEY ANNE WILLIAMS, born 1944, USA

THE HOUSE OF DESIRE

I

This is really the story of a
sista who was very too-ga-tha
in everythang but life. You
see she was so too-ga-tha
she had nothang but
strife. Everyone thought

because she was so
too-ga-tha she didn't
feel pain and the men she went
with felt just the same. They got
to-gatha with her and then, once they
were, left in most un-togatha ways.

Her end was a black one without pain,
tears of strife. She finally
concluded there's no earthly
use in bein too-ga-tha
if it don't put some
joy in yo
life.

▮▮ JENNY JOSEPH, born 1932, UK

WARNING

When I am an old woman I shall wear purple
With a red hat which doesn't go, and doesn't suit me.
And I shall spend my pension on brandy and summer gloves
And satin sandals, and say we've no money for butter.
I shall sit down on the pavement when I'm tired
And gobble up samples in shops and press alarm bells

And run my stick along the public railings
And make up for the sobriety of my youth.
I shall go out in my slippers in the rain
And pick the flowers in other people's gardens
And learn to spit.

You can wear terrible shirts and grow more fat
And eat three pounds of sausages at a go
Or only bread and pickle for a week
And hoard pens and pencils and beermats and things in
    boxes.

But now we must have clothes that keep us dry
And pay our rent and not swear in the street
And set a good example for the children.
We must have friends to dinner and read the papers.

But maybe I ought to practise a little now?
So people who know me are not too shocked or surprised
When suddenly I am old, and start to wear purple.

**// ZINDZISWA MANDELA (at twelve years),
South Africa**

MY COUNTRY
For Mandela

I stand by the gate
School's out
Smoke fills the location
Tears come to my eyes

I wipe them away
I walk into the kitchen
To see my mother's
Black hard-washing hands
A forceful smile from
A tired face

We sit and have supper
I pick up a picture of
My father and look
My mother turns away
Tries to hide

My father left my mother
In his arms
He is roughly separated
From her

The van pulls away
Mother watches bravely enough
I as a child do
Not understand

My heart aches
How I long to see my father
At least to hold his hand
And comfort him
Or at least to tell him
He'll be back some day

// MARY WILSON, UK

MAMZELLE

The Summer Term had just begun;
My desk was warm beneath the sun;
I leaned across the window ledge
To smell the springing sweet-briar hedge.
The quiet garden seemed to wait;
I heard a footstep by the gate,
Across the grass a shadow fell –
   I looked – and saw Mamzelle.

My mouth is dry as she goes by —
One curving line from foot to thigh —
And, with unEnglish liberty
Her bosom bounces, full and free;
Pale skin, pink lips, a wide blue stare,
Her page-boy fall of silky hair
Swings on her shoulders like a bell;
   O how I love Mamzelle!

She cannot get her idioms right,
She weeps for Paris in the night
Or, in the tension of the Match,
She laughs when someone drops a catch!
The other staff are not unkind
But distant; she tries not to mind,
And I would gladly go through Hell
   Just to protect Mamzelle.

On Conversation Walks we go,
I touch her sleeve — she doesn't know;
All summer's beauty round her lies
As 'Parlez Français, girls!' she cries.
I do not smile, I do not talk,
In silence by her side I walk
And hope that no one there can tell
   How much I love Mamzelle.

The sunny days are hurrying past;
Their painful sweetness will not last;
The poppies burn among the hay,
The heartless cuckoo sings all day;
The Home Farm woods are green and cool,
There's laughter from the swimming pool.
At end-of-term I say farewell
   For ever to Mamzelle.

Perhaps I shall forget her face,
Her gentleness, her body's grace;
Even her accents, deep and slow,
May be forgotten. And I know
That I, throughout the coming years,
May love with joy, may love with tears;
But shall I ever love so well
  As now I love Mamzelle?

// CHERYL CLARKE, born 1947, USA

IF YOU BLACK GET BACK

Vashti
with her one brown
and one hazel eye
was an ugly and dirty little black girl
whose nappy hair could not hold a curl
whose name nobody even wanted to say
much less to play
with her
so in awe of browns and tans we were.

Vashti
with her hard hazel eye
was dull in school
but broke no rule.
Teachers laughed openly at her stutter,
frequently calling upon her to read aloud.
Cowed, her face swelling like an udder,
she would rise to the effort
and the humiliation.

Vashti's hair was never straightened.
To be black was bad enough.
To be black and have nappy hair
was just plain rough.

Boys terrorized her.
Girls scorned her.
Adults walked the other way
to avoid the play
of Vashti's eyes
marking their cruelty.

So black she could stand out in a coal bin.
So black she was most nearly blue.
So black it was a sin.
So black she could stop the dew.
Vashti learned to live
and love with pain.
Wore it like a coat of armor
rather resembling an armadillo.

// U. A. FANTHORPE, UK

GROWING UP

I wasn't good
At being a baby. Burrowed my way
Through the long yawn of infancy,
Masking by instinct how much I knew
Of the senior world, sabotaging
As far as I could, biding my time,
Biting my rattle, my brother (in private),
Shoplifting daintily into my pram.
Not a good baby,
No.

I wasn't good
At being a child. I missed
The innocent age. Children,
Being childish, were beneath me.
Adults I despised or distrusted. They
Would label my every disclosure

Precocious, naïve, whatever it was.
I disdained definition, preferred to be surly.
Not a nice child,
No.

I wasn't good
At adolescence. There was a dance,
A catchy rhythm; I was out of step.
My body capered, nudging me
With hairy, fleshy growths and monthly outbursts,
To join the party. I tried to annul
The future, pretended I knew it already,
Was caught bloody-thighed, a criminal
Guilty of puberty.
Not a nice girl,
No.

(My hero, intransigent Emily,
Cauterized her own-dog-mauled
Arm with a poker,
Struggled to die on her feet,
Never told anyone anything.)

I wasn't good
At growing up. Never learned
The natives' art of life. Conversation
Disintegrated as I touched it,
So I played mute, wormed along years,
Reciting the hard-learned arcane litany
Of cliché, my company passport.
Not a nice person,
No.

The gift remains
Masonic, dark. But age affords
A vocation even for wallflowers.
Called to be connoisseur, I collect,
Admire, the effortless bravura
Of other people's lives, proper and comely,
Treading the measure, shopping, chaffing,
Quarrelling, drinking, not knowing

How right they are, or how, like well-oiled bolts,
Swiftly and sweet, they slot into the grooves
Their ancestors smoothed out along the grain.

// JEAN TEPPERMAN, born 1945, USA

WITCH

They told me
I smile prettier with my mouth closed.
They said —
better cut your hair —
long, it's all frizzy,
looks Jewish.
They hushed me in restaurants
looking around them
while the mirrors above the table
jeered infinite reflections
of a raw, square face.
They questioned me
when I sang in the street.
They stood taller at tea
smoothly explaining
my eyes on the saucers,
trying to hide the hand grenade
in my pants pocket,
or crouched behind the piano.
They mocked me with magazines
full of breasts and lace,
published their triumph
when the doctor's oldest son
married a nice sweet girl.
They told me tweed-suit stories
of various careers of ladies.
I woke up at night
afraid of dying.
They built screens and room dividers

to hide unsightly desire
sixteen years old
raw and hopeless
they buttoned me into dresses
covered with pink flowers.
They waited for me to finish
then continued the conversation.
I have been invisible,
weird and supernatural.
I want my black dress.
I want my hair
curling wild around me.
I want my broomstick
from the closet where I hid it.
Tonight I meet my sisters
in the graveyard.
Around midnight
if you stop at a red light
in the wet city traffic,
watch for us against the moon.
We are screaming,
we are flying,
laughing, and won't stop.

NURUNNESSA CHOUDHURY, born 1943, Bangladesh
(translated by Nurunnessa Choudhury and Paul Joseph Thompson)

THE SUN WITNESS

Long ago a young girl
wearing a saffron-coloured saree
walked gracefully
on her way –
She moved the square stone
from the white
near-dead grass.
By the lightning speed
of her black hand.

Silently, with her gaze,
she commanded the sun
to send its light
down upon everything,
even the white grass.

The sun accepted
her easy command
and came down with humility.

Days after
she passed beggars in the street,
and tucked in her silk saree
to avoid their stains.

Seeing this,
the sun hid behind clouds,
and rain came,
unexpectedly, like tears.

▟▟ SUSAN WALLBANK, born 1943, UK

INVITATION TO A DANCE

Thirty years ago we stood in rows
sex facing sex across a wooden floor
At the command of 'Go' the broken needle falls
into a foxtrot quickstep or slow waltz
The enemy advances breaking rank
some fast to grasp intended flesh but others
slower and more hesitant, afraid
of being made a fool, afraid of friends or friendless
and afraid of going home again alone.

Girls did not have to walk across the wood
exposed to ridicule and moving through a flack
of adolescent repartee and wit
and many a sniper's bullet hit its Mark
or John or Clive and left him dying there
beneath the foxtrot quickstep or slow waltz.

And now I go alone again to parties
less formalised the sexes intermix
and listening the words flow fast as drink
and food provides a small safe place
to sink into a chair and think of nothing,
to watch each separate dancer dance untouched
with no waltz now to bind them into pairs.

The gap between the sexes is still there
and only fools and drunken horses dare
to cross it. Three decades on I sit
exposed to hope, still as a photograph
and silent as a sphinx, flower-scented
gun at the ready, bayonet fully fixed
and wait patiently for someone to come.

// NANCY MOREJÓN, born 1944, Cuba
(translated by Kathleen Weaver)

RICHARD BROUGHT HIS FLUTE

III

The day the two old women were dissecting two birds
in the back-room of some museum
we came home drained
wanting only to hear some jazz
happiness was all in the pleasure of listening
    held in the sway of magic

for me it was the first time
the first time
the first I ever heard a clarinet so fierce
   so smoky
   so heated
thanks to Grandfather Egües an era had begun for us
childhood revived
   and begun again

only that clarinet like a bridge
and the coppery glance of Gladys
a few pounds heavier
we hung on every breath
the dust-caked needle tracking

Mozart and Europe laughed in the far distance
while we were desperately dancing
to a kettledrum bass a trumpet
flute percussion gourd
all playing together
the drumbeats leaping out of the same fire

it was the first time the great first time
and all silence was reduced to listening

// SANDY McINTOSH, Jamaica

LOST, ONE SOUL

I lost my soul in a fit of temper
I threw it at somebody's head
and slammed out
without a second thought

Then I dumped it in a wastebin
along with a love I said I was finished with

I sandpapered my spirit
with a million
bitter barbs
and sent it into orbit
and substituted
guilt instead

My soul went cold
with memories of old friends and kin
who never expected
to be neglected,
and resolutions
I'd eluded

Then one day
I went to feed it
and it was gone
and now I hear it howling
in the wind outside
in the nights
in the hills

and I get the chills inside

and hide
in something that's not important
and it's four in the morning
before I can get warm enough
to weep enough
to fall asleep

ANNA MARIA LENNGREN, 1754–1819, Sweden
(translated from Swedish by Nadia Christensen and Marianne Tiblin)

OTHER FABRICS, OTHER MORES!

'When I was young,' said Aunt to me,
'Women then, about the year
Seventeen-thirty, Betty dear,
Dressed in decent linsey woolsey!
No painted faces would one find,
Nor flimsy gowns on womenfolk.
The fairer sex possessed a mind
Of sturdy fabric, like a cloak.
Now all is different in our lives –
Other fabrics, other mores!
Taffetas, indecent stories
Of young girls as well as wives!
The path of lust they boldly walk;
Shameless manners, daring ways,
Make-up, muslins, brazen talk
Go hand-in-hand with modern days.'

NIKKI GIOVANNI, born 1943, America

NIKKI ROSA

childhood memories are always a drag
if you're Black
you always remember things like living in Woodlawn
with no inside toilet
and if you become famous or something
they never talk about how happy you were to have
your mother
all to yourself and
how good the water felt when you got your bath
from one of those
big tubs that folk in chicago barbeque in

14

and somehow when you talk about home
it never gets across how much you
understood their feelings
as the whole family attended meetings about Hollydale
and even though you remember
your biographers never understand
your father's pain as he sells his stock
and another dream goes
And though you're poor it isn't poverty that
concerns you
and though they fought a lot
it isn't your father's drinking that makes any difference
but only that everybody is together and you
and your sister have happy birthdays and very good
Christmases
and I really hope no white person ever has cause
to write about me
because they'll never understand
Black love is Black wealth and they'll
probably talk about my hard childhood
and never understand that
all the while I was quite happy

▐▐ MARY LONNBERG SMITH, USA

CARTWHEELS

We never laughed much:
there was something solemn
about your mother's gleaming kitchen, the cake
displayed like a rare museum piece
under its plastic dome.
Though we spent afternoons reading comics,
practicing cartwheels on your sunny lawn,
and making up rhymes about the boys we knew,
I was almost relieved to go home.

Your mother was tight-lipped, disapproving,
older than anyone else's mother,
and when she took her long leap
into the bay, I avoided you.
I could not step across the lawn
where we did our acrobatics
without the sudden vision of your mother
turning slow, silent cartwheels through the fog.

▗▖ NOÉMIA DA SOUSA, born 1927, Mozambique
(translated from Portuguese by Kathleen Weaver and Allan Francovich)

POEM OF DISTANT CHILDHOOD

When I was born in the great house on the bank of the sea
It was midday and the sun shone on the Indian ocean.
Sea gulls hovered, white, drunk with blue.
The boats of the Indian fishermen had not yet returned
dragging the overloaded nets.
On the bridge, the cries of the blacks, the blacks of the boats
calling to the married women melting in the heat —
bundles on their heads, street urchins at their sides —
the cries sounded like a long song,
long, suspended in the fog of the silence.
And on the scalding steps
beggar Mufasini slept, in a swarm of flies.

When I was born . . .
I know the air was calm, still (they told me)
and the sun shone on the sea.
In the midst of this calm I was launched in the world,
already with my stigma.
And I cried and screamed, I don't know why.
Ah, but for the life outside,
my tears dried in the light of revolt.
And the sun never again shone as in the first days
of my existence

although the brilliant maritime scenery of my childhood,
constantly calm, like a marsh,
always guided my adolescent steps –
my stigma too.
And even more, the mixed companions of my childhood.

Companions
fishing under the bridge with a pin hook and line of thin wire
my ragged friends with stomachs round as baskets
companions running and jumping in the bush and
beaches of Catembe
together in the marvellous discovery of the nest of the
    warblers
in the construction of a columned snare
with the sticky sap of the wild fig tree
in the hunt for hummingbirds and blue-headed lizards,
and chasing monkeys under a burning summer sun.
Unforgettable figures as I grew up –
Free, happy children:
black, mulatto, white, Indian,
sons of the baker and black washerwoman,
of the black man of the boats and the carpenter,
come from the misery of Guachene
or the wooden houses of fishermen.
Coddled children from the post,
smart-aleck sons of the customs guards of Esquadrilla
comrades in the always new adventure
of assaults on the cashew tree in the vegetable gardens,
companions in the secret of the sweetest cones of the pine,
and in the eerie chill of the 'Island of Lost Ships',
where every sound makes an echo.

Oh my companions, crouched, amazed in the marvellous
gathering of the 'Karingana wa karingana'
the stories of the old women of Portugal
in the terrible storm-black sunsets
(the wind shrieking in the zinc roof,
the sea menacing the wooden steps of the veranda,
the causeway groaning, groaning,
inconsolably

and filling our souls with strange, inexplicable fears,
our souls full of toothless spirits
and Massinga kings turned hunchbacked . . .)
Yes, my companions sowed in me the seed of this
    dissatisfaction
day by day I grow more dissatisfied.
They filled my childhood with the sun that shone
on the day I was born.
With their luminous unthinking comradeship,
their radiant happiness,
their explosive enthusiasm before any winged kite
in the technicolor blue of the sky,
their immediate, unconditional loyalty –
they filled my childhood
with unforgettable happiness and adventure.

If today the sun does not shine
as on the day I was born
in the great house by the Indian Ocean,
I will not let myself sleep in darkness.
My companions are sure guides
on my life's path
They prove that 'brotherhood' is not a mere pretty word
written in black in the bookcase dictionary:
They showed me that brotherhood is a beautiful thing and is
    possible
even when skins and surrounding landscapes
differ so much.

So I BELIEVE that one day
the sun will shine again, calm, on the Indian Ocean.
Sea gulls will hover, white, drunk with blue
and the fishermen will return singing,
sailing on the tenuous afternoon.
And this poison of the moon that suffering has infused in my
veins will cease disturbing me for ever.
One day,
life will be flooded with sun.
And it will be like a new childhood shining for everyone . . .

NURUNNESSA CHOUDHURY, born 1943, Bangladesh
(translated by Nurunnessa Choudhury and Paul Joseph Thompson)

BLUE SPECKS

In the clear world
I blew a cage of glass
and hid myself inside.
Like a lonely child
I played with words —
thoughts,
special thoughts,
which I would
make, then break,
saying
no — not now — not yet.
The fire of spring
scorched my heart and body.
I achieved awareness
of life's bass and treble notes:
I trapped wonder
and asked:
What is it?
Saying
no — not now — not yet.
Then, in darkness,
stormswept, you came.
Next day
I took apart the cage,
smashed the glass
and gave it to the sky:
This was your gift.
I picked up
my faithless heart,
and met the world
with direct gaze.

◢◢ MAHSATI, twelfth century, Iran
(translated from Farsi by Deirdre Lashgari)

QUATRAINS

Better to live as a rogue and a bum,
    a lover all treat as a joke,
to hang out with a crowd of comfortable drunks,
    than crouch in a hypocrite's cloak.

Unless you can dance through a common bar
    with a vagabond's step, you're not going to make it.
This is the road of the reckless who gamble
    their lives; risk yours, or you're not going to make it.

◢◢ JULIA VINOGRAD, USA

I HATE POETRY

I hate poetry
the way a junky hates the fix
he can't afford
and will have to hustle for
and often enough
won't even get a rush from,
just keep off the horrors
for another hour.
I hate poetry
the way a married couple
who don't believe in divorce
hate each other.
I hate poetry
the way Alcoholics Anonymous
hates liquor
and has meetings about it.

I hate poetry
the way an atheist hates God
and shakes his fist
at the empty hole in the sky.
And the more poetry I hear
the more I hate it
and the more I write it.
Here I am.

◢◢ ALICE WALKER, born 1944, USA

I SAID TO POETRY

I said to Poetry: 'I'm finished
with you.'
Having to almost die
before some weird light
comes creeping through
is no fun.
'No thank you, Creation,
no muse need apply.
I'm out for good times –
at the very least,
some painless convention.

Poetry laid back
and played dead
until this morning.
I wasn't sad or anything,
only restless.

Poetry said: 'You remember
the desert, and how glad you were
that you have an eye
to see it with? You remember
that, if ever so slightly?'
I said: 'I didn't hear that.
Besides, it's five o'clock in the a.m.

I'm not getting up
in the dark
to talk to you.'

Poetry said: 'But think about the time
you saw the moon
over that small canyon
that you liked much better
than the grand one — and how surprised you were
that the moonlight was green
and you still had
one good eye
to see it with.

Think of that!'

'I'll join the church!' I said,
huffily, turning my face to the wall.
'I'll learn how to pray again!'

'Let me ask you,' said Poetry.
'When you pray, what do you think
you'll see?'

Poetry had me.

'There's no paper
in this room,' I said.
'And that new pen I bought
makes a funny noise.'

'Bullshit,' said Poetry.
'Bullshit,' said I.

// **MARIA BANUS, born 1914, Romania**
(translated by Laura Schiff and Dana Beldiman)

THE NEW NOTEBOOK

Full of superstition
I begin a new notebook,
white leaves – sea foam.
I close my eyes and wait
for the first day of the world,
for Aphrodite with wet lips,
red curls of flame,
an open shell,
shy and sure,
to rise from the salt foam,
out of the primordial algae.
I wait under closed eyelids.
One can hear the grey rustle of sea gulls
under the low sky
and the monotonous thunder of waves
only of waves
which come and go.

// **CHIRLANE McCRAY, twentieth century**

I USED TO THINK

I used to think
I can't be a poet
because a poem is being everything you can be
in one moment
speaking with lightning protest
unveiling a fiery intellect
or letting the words drift feather-soft
into the ears of strangers
who will suddenly understand
my beautiful and tortured soul.

But, I've spent my life as a black girl,
a nappy-headed, no haired,
fat lipped
big-bottomed Black girl
and the poem will surely come out wrong
like me.
And I don't want everyone looking at me.
If I could be a cream coloured lovely
with gypsy curls,
someone's pecan dream and sweet sensation,
I'd be poetry in motion
without saying a word
and wouldn't have to make sense if I did.
If I were beautiful, I could be angry and cute
instead of an evil, pouting mammy bitch
a nigger woman, passed over
conquested and passed over,
a nigger woman
to do it in the bushes.
My mother tells me
I used to run home crying
that I wanted to be light like my sisters
She shook her head and told me
there was nothing wrong with my colour.
She didn't tell me I was pretty
(so my head wouldn't swell up)
Black girls can't afford to
have illusions of grandeur
not ass-kicking, too-loud-laughing
mean and loose black girls.
And even though in Afrika
I was mistaken for someone's fine
sister or cousin, or neighbour down the way
even though I swore
never again to walk with my head down
ashamed
never to care
that those people who celebrate
the popular brand of beauty

don't see me
it still matters.
Looking for a job, it matters.
Standing next to my lover
when someone light gets that
'she ain't nothing come home with me'
it matters.
But it's not so bad now
I can laugh about it,
trade stories and write poems
about all those put downs
my rage and hiding,
I'm through waiting for
minds to change
The '60s didn't put me on a throne
and as many
years as I've been
Black like ebony
Black like the night
I have seen in the mirror
and the eyes of my sisters
that pretty is the
woman in darkness
who flowers with loving.

// MARGARET RECKORD, Jamaica

AMA CREDO

Needing
to go separate
along my green homings
barefoot to the thud
of fruit falling
solitaire calling
my compass, lodestar
glinting upmountain

hemmed in with pineneedles
canopied with sunsets
flaming me steeds
to stride
across sky on;
world softening
to mist
mornings shaking open
blue tablecloths
for me
to write big
and brief
on.

// MRIRIDA N'AIT ATTIK, twentieth century, Morocco
(translated into French by René Euloge; English version by Daniel Halpern
   and Paula Paley)

MRIRIDA

They nicknamed me Mririda.
Mririda, nimble tree-frog of the meadow.
I don't have her gold eyes,
I don't have her white throat
Or green tunic.
But what I have, like Mririda,
Is my zezarit, my call
That carries up to the sheepfolds –
The whole valley
And the other side of the mountain
Speak of it . . .
My call, which brings astonishment and envy.

They named me Mririda
Because the first time I walked in the fields
I gently took a tree-frog,
Afraid and trembling in my hands,
And pressed her white throat
To my lips of a child,
And then of a girl.

And so I was given the baraka,
The magic that gives them their song
Which fills the summer nights,
A song clear as glass,
Sharp as the sound of an anvil
In the vibrating air before rain . . .

Because of this gift
They call me Mririda,
And he who will come for me
Will feel my heart beat in his hand
As I have felt the racing hearts of frogs
Beneath my fingertips.

In the nights bathed in moonlight
He will call me, Mririda, Mririda,
Sweet nickname that I love,
And for him I will release my piercing call,
Shrill and drawn out,
Bringing wonder from men
And jealousy from women,
Nothing like it ever heard in this valley.

SHO NUFF

Cold soft drinks
quenched my thirst
one hot and humid July day
after a cool drive
to a mountain store.
Seems like every woman
in the place
had on halter tops
displaying their expensive tans.
There were two women
standing in front of me
at the checkout counter.
One said to the other,
'You must be a lady of leisure,
just look at your beautiful tan.'
Then the other woman responded,
'No, you must be a lady of leisure,
yours is much darker than mine.'
A tall dark and handsome Black dude
standing behind me
whispering down my Black back
s
   a
     i
       d
'Sister, if those two
are ladies of leisure,
you must surely be
a lady of royalty.'
And in a modest tone, I replied,
'SHO NUFF?'

TAIWO OLALEYE-ORUENE, born Nigeria

AFRICAN BEAUTY

Who say we no get beauty for Africa
Abi de pers'n dey craze
Abi e dey blind sef

Wetin pass fine like African lady
Wetin be elegant
Like African woman in bubu
Or in iro and buba
Abi na wrapper sef
Whosai una go see beauty
Like African woman in plaits
Whosai una go see natural beauty
Like African woman
Wey no wear make-up
Wey no wan copy oyinbo
Wey be proud of im color

Una see anything wey pass grace
Like an African lady
Wey, dress in up and down
E dey move like gazelle
De figure
Weder na slender e be
Weder na mama figure e get
De whistles no dey stop
De go slow for road be plenty
Na so de moto dey stop for road
De men in de oborku
Abi na rover
Or efen jaguar sef
Dey wan dis African beauty
De men wan dis epitome of African womanhood
De prize of Africa
For de African beauty
Na a true African

MAGALY SÁNCHEZ, born 1940, Cuba
(translated by Margaret Randall)

ALMOST LOVE

It happen sometimes; a pair of eyes a profile
someone we don't know and see only once
or every afternoon.
Someone we met, it was just like that:
a hand on yours
some hasty words.
But someone who became a part of you
and now there's no seeing that face without paling
without trembling hands
and it's almost love.

NANCY MOREJÓN, born 1944, Cuba
(translated by Kathleen Weaver)

TO A BOY

Between sea-foam and the tide
his back rises
while afternoon in solitude
went down.

I held his black eyes, like grasses
among brown Pacific shells.

I held his fine lips
like a salt boiling in the sands.

I held, at last, his incense-chin
under the sun.

A boy of the world over me
and Biblical songs
modeled his legs, his ankles
and the grapes of his sex
and the raining hymns that sprang
from his mouth
entwining us like two seafarers
lashed to the uncertain sails of love.

In his arms, I live.
In his hard arms I longed to die
like a wet bird.

// DINAH LIVINGSTONE, UK

DESIRE

Night after night
beached mer mammal,
kin to seal and dolphin,
she lies on her belly
and cries for the sea:
'Oh cover me, cover me,
my element, my delight.
Why do you never
kiss me under this moon?

I do not walk on knives
for an alien popinjay.
My pearly tail flaps,
I crave my salt love.
Oh cover me, cover me.
I am a large creature,
I am a load of desire,
unburden me of my sorrow.

My round breasts
press into the sand,
I scratch, I twitch, I am wet.
But my heart is parched,
I am ache, am empty,
will you not fill me?
The crests of the waves are foamy,
he is strong and eager,
I hear him coming.

Oh reach me quickly.
Do not abandon me
on this moon-bleached beach.
Dissolve me, cover me,
mighty, lovable Neptune,
hold me, supple and light,
I exult, I somersault.
Now take me, take me now.'

▰▰ TERESITA FERNÁNDEZ, born 1930, Cuba
(translated by Margaret Randall)

EVERY DAY THAT I LOVE YOU

Each day's morning tastes of thinking of you,
I go out to dust the carnations, to check the violets,
to cut the last small rose.

Autumn begins to decorate the ground
with its fragile bits of loosened gold.
I'm happy there are flowers small enough
to fit the heart of a letter . . .

Each autumn day the sky tries out a grey
that brings me sadness . . .
Sometimes it rains . . .
and the street noises stop. Sometimes.
Then I listen to me say I love you . . .

On days like that people penetrate the innocence
sleeping in the depths of eyes . . .
Each day I love you
our tiny quota of beauty takes its place in time.

▮▮ HUANG HO, 1498–1569, China
(translated by Kenneth Rexroth and Ling Chung)

TO THE TUNE 'A FLOATING CLOUD CROSSES ENCHANTED MOUNTAIN'

Every morning I get up
Beautiful as the Goddess
Of love in Enchanted Mountain.
Every night I go to bed
Seductive as Yang Kuei-fei,
The imperial concubine.
My slender waist and thighs
Are exhausted and weak
From a night of cloud dancing.
But my eyes are still lewd,
And my cheeks are flushed.
My old wet nurse combs
My cloud-like hair.
My lover, fragrant as incense,
Adjusts my jade hairpins, and
Draws on my silk stockings
Over my feet and legs
Perfumed with orchids;
And once again we fall over
Overwhelmed with passion.

▟▟ VILLANA (between 900 and 1100), India
(translated from Sanskrit by Willis Barnstone)

Poem untitled

After he stripped off my clothes,
unable to cover my breasts with my thin arms
I clung to his chest as to my robe.
But when his hand crept below my hips,
who could save me from plunging into a sea of shame
but the love god
who teaches us how to faint?

▟▟ NINA CASSIAN, born 1924, Romania
(translated by Laura Schiff)

THANKS

I can't take it – you're so handsome!
And when night falls your hair shimmers
grand and tragic like the echo
of blood on a shield.
Your eyes make the air pulse,
they electrify the house,
the drawers open, rugs flood
down the stairs like a river.
Your star-like teeth
rip open my heart like lightning.
I can't stand it – you're too much!

But look, thanks for your low forehead.
It gives me more leisure to spend
on those beautiful lips, those treacherous teeth.

34

JENNIFER BROWN, Jamaica

AFRICA AND THE CARIBBEAN

I came to you
fresh
dew wet
child of these islands
jewel of the Caribbean Sea
and you loved
my skin
like black sand beaches;
my hair
like coconut fibres
my lips
large and generous
tasting of sun and fruit.
You took me home
and together we dug
until we found
my long lost navel string;
we recalled the ceremonies
that had subsided in my skin;
I sang for you
my new songs
and we slept together at dawn.

TINA REID, UK

HE MAY BE A PHOTOGRAPH OF HIMSELF

He is beautiful and still
And unmarked from within,
A mountain in winter,
A loch at dusk.

I sat in his lee
Sharpening flints,
Words to lead
The assault on his rock-face.

I stood on his shore,
Hurling stone
After stone
And did not break his surface.

It will take a disaster,
A mining enterprise,
A dam-burst,
Or a betrayal

To show him,
To know him,
To see the change
I made.

▟▟ MARY DORCEY, born 1950, Eire

RETURN

At last, the train will lurch in,
twenty minutes past the hour, the
dark flesh of the hills, heaved behind
before us, the narrowing fields,
the layered clouds, drifting
beyond us, lit for some other advent.
And everything will conspire
against me: luggage and children
crowding the aisle. A white-haired
woman, home from England,

Awkward with haste, will labour
her case to the door, her floral
print dress, a last check between me
and my first glimpse of you.
And there you are – by the turnstile
I will see you come through, though you
miss me; your brilliant eyes in flight
along the carriage windows.
You will wear your red, linen shirt,
the sleeves turned back, and snatched

From the hedges as you drove,
a swathe of flowers in your arms.
(Such a trail strewn behind us – a trail
of departures and pardons.) And my
blood will betray me – the old response,
I will hesitate, as if there might
still be time to change course,
or simply, not wanting to be caught
waiting for your gaze? The sky
will shift as I step out, a handful

Of sun thrust down on your hair.
On the narrow platform, our hips
will draw close, we will not mind
how they stare – the aggrieved faces –
such a fuss for a woman!
And in that moment, your laughter,
the heat of your neck at my mouth,
it will all be behind me again
I swear, as though coming home,
as though for the first time.

⫽ KATH FRASER, UK

SONG (OCTOBER 1969)

I love you, Mrs Acorn. Would your husband mind
if I kissed you under the autumn sun,
if my brown-leaf guilty passion made you blind
to his manly charms and fun?

I want you, Mrs Acorn. Do you think you'll come
to see my tangled, windswept desires,
and visit me in my everchanging house of some
vision of winter's fires?

I am serious, Mrs Acorn, do you hear?
Forget your family and other ties,
Come with me to where there is no fear,
where we'll find summer butterflies.

I am serious, Mrs Acorn, are you deaf?

*I now realise, with the raising of general awareness of the politics around
disabilities since I wrote the poem in 1969, that the last line may sound
offensive to women who are hard of hearing. For this I apologise. Kath Fraser*

⫽ AUDRE LORDE, born, 1934, USA

ON A NIGHT OF THE FULL MOON

I
Out of my flesh that hungers
and my mouth that knows
comes the shape I am seeking
for reason.
The curve of your waiting body
fits my waiting hand
your breasts warm as sunlight
your lips quick as young birds
between your thighs the sweet
sharp taste of limes.

Thus I hold you
frank in my heart's eye
in my skin's knowing
as my fingers conceive your flesh
I feel your stomach
moving against me.

Before the moon wanes again
we shall come together.

II
And I would be the moon
spoken over your beckoning flesh
breaking against reservations
beaching thought
my hands at your high tide
over and under inside you
and the passing of hungers
attended, forgotten.

Darkly risen
the moon speaks
my eyes
judging your roundness
delightful.

// MARY DORCEY, born 1950, Eire

SEA CHANGE

Your thighs your belly —
their sweep and strength —
your breasts so sudden;
nipples budding in my hands,
the sheen of your back
under my palms
your flanks smooth as flame.

Your skin – that inner skin
like silk,
your mouth deepening
full as an orchid
honey on my tongue.

The dizzy lurch and sway –
seaflowers under water;
changing skins with every touch
and then and again, that voice
– your voice, breaking over me,
opening earth with its call
and rocking the moon in her tide.

// ALICE WALKER, born 1944, USA

NEW FACE

I have learned not to worry about love;
but to honor its coming
with all my heart.
To examine the dark mysteries
of the blood
with headless heed and
swirl,
to know the rush of feelings
swift and flowing
as water.
The source appears to be
some inexhaustible
spring
within our twin and triple
selves;
the new face I turn up
to you
no one else on earth
has ever
seen.

GILLIAN E. HANSCOMBE, born 1945, Australia

FROM FIVE LOVESICK POEMS

IV
From her grave

she sends incense.

From her grave

she sends candles.

From her grave

she sends trinkets.

From her grave

she sends echoes.

From her grave

she sends prophecies.

From her grave

she sends fire.

in the fissure of my lips

I bake and eat it.

in the basin of my hands

I wear them in my hair.

at the stern of my eyes

I dispose them.

on the outcrop of my words

I rehearse them.

at the source of my dreams

I inscribe their intent.

at the keel of my fears

I devour it with my lover.

◢◢ AUDRE LORDE, born 1934, USA

MEMORIAL I

If you come as softly
as wind within the trees
you may hear what I hear
see what sorrow sees.

If you come as lightly
as the threading dew
I shall take you gladly
nor ask more of you.

You may sit beside me
silent as a breath
and only those who stay dead
shall remember death.

If you come I will be silent
nor speak harsh words to you –
I will not ask you why, now,
nor how, nor what you knew.

But we shall sit here softly
beneath two different years
and the rich earth between us
shall drink our tears.

◢◢ CHRISTINE CRAIG, Jamaica

FOR D. S.

Once the stone god turned its
marble eyes and breathed out
moonlit fire on my thoughts.
Once I saw a river born, thrown
free from veins of chalky earth.

Once I even saw an egret
white throat stretched, swallow
the sunset all in one gulp.

But once, behind your sheltered eyes
I saw a flower curving from your palm.

// MAUREEN BURGE, UK

DISILLUSION

Look at him, over there
Watch him turn his head and stare
I think he fancies me

See the way he turns around
See him look me up and down
I'm sure he fancies me

Look at his lovely jet black hair
I don't really like 'em fair
I just know he fancies me

He's coming over, aint he great
He's gonna ask me for a date
I knew he fancied me

Hang on just a minute though
He's heading straight for my mate Flo
And I thought he fancied me

Tara Flo, I'll go on home
I spose I really should have known
He didn't fancy me

I don't like un anyway
He's ugly
I don't fancy he

▟▟ DINAH BUTLER, born 1960, UK

DO YOU FANCY ME?

Do you fancy me?
Your talent is worthy like purple.
Do you see the same in me
undisciplined, dilute perhaps
but there?
Would your prick salute in recognition
and make me worthy?

Do you fancy me?
You orate a realm to rule
chasten the riotous outrage of arguments
come scaling your walls,
decimate the enemy who wield them.
Would my pass words
let me in to hug a gap of you
where rage recedes and
your anger scalds the middle distance?
Would you hold me close as
blameless balm?
And as our eyes meet,
I offer earnestness.
Reassured, you look on past
towards the sea of challengers.

Do you fancy me?
Do I suit and do I
meet with your approval
and requirements?
Will you endorse my thoughts?
Will you turn these
simple breasts to beauty
beneath your gaze?
Am I a winner? Do I win that
stirring in your groin?

Could I become
your life's pin-up and find
myself a face?
So
do you fancy me?
Well I am sick of it.

░░ MARGARET RANDALL, born 1936, USA

EVER NOTICE HOW IT IS WITH WOMEN?

The guy asked me
Hey, what time you have?
And I looked at my watch
and I told him.
Five to ten.

Five to ten, hey!
That's right!
And he looked at his own watch
– I hadn't noticed –
and confirmed by his authority
I was 'right'.

Ever notice how it is with women
he said then to a guy on my right
How they're always ten minutes fast
five minutes slow –

Yeah, the other guy shoots back,
and my eyes moved from one to the other,
Guess it's to help them
get places on time,
you know how it is,
and my eyes move from one to the other,
they're talking about me
not to me but about me
through me

about women 'in general'
me in general.

Can I be in-general?
Collective, yes,
one of my people, yes,
but in-general?

I'm not there,
the answers are always pain
and much too later.
Now it's just my eyes
moving from one to the other
momentarily blinded

by this newest form
of male chauvinist bullshit.

// MARGE PIERCY, USA

THE MEANINGFUL EXCHANGE

The man talks
the woman listens

The man is a teapot
with a dark green brew
of troubles.
He pours into the woman.
She carries his sorrows away
sloshing in her belly.

The man swings off lighter.
Sympathy quickens him.
He watches women pass.
He whistles.

The woman lumbers away.
Inside his troubles are
snaking up through her throat.
Her body curls delicately
about them, worrying, nudging
them into some new meaningful shape
squatting now at the centre of her life.

How much lighter I feel,
the man says, ready
for business.
How heavy I feel, the woman
says: this must be love.

▮▮ ANON., traditional, Morocco
(translated by Willis Barnstone)

AN ANCIENT SONG OF A WOMAN OF FEZ

I see a man who is dull
and boring like no one else.

He is heavier than massive mountains.
When he laughs he shakes the plains of Gharb,
when he cries the coastal cities tremble.

To look at an ugly man
gives me a headache.

DRY ROCK NUMBER

He's lean
He's clean

He's bony
He's stony

He's spare
He's bare

I want to grow his cock
Until it breaks into flower
Wild roses Dog roses

I want a garden in his face
Mountains in his eyes
And rivers coursing through his hair

But all he does is come
and go
And he goes
Even faster than he comes

He's a flower
Under glass

He's a scream
In a box

He's a lark
On crutches

I want to green his intestine
And cultivate his kidneys
See his liver spring into leaf

I want to silver birch his skin
Weave willows of his limbs
And climb into his heart of oak

But all he does is come
And go
And he goes
Even faster than he comes

He doesn't know
Who can show

Make him see
Never me

The next one.
Maybe.

DAZZLY ANDERSON, UK

SOME MEN

Wee nah look no quarrel wi dem
Wee a get old, wee need some peace
Lord, pain a take over wee head
Lord help wee before dem kill us

A meck dem a treat wee so bad
You get up every day, dem treat you like a dog
Wee a get old, wee need some peace
Wee hair a get grey, wi all deh worries

Woman ha heavy load fi carry
Deh man dem meck sure a dat
You can say noting
Dem ready fi use dem hand pon yu

Lord a wha do deh men dem so
Dem teck over your body
But dem no satisfied
Dem want teck over yu life too

Dem treat you like a little pickney
Lord a wha do deh men dem so
Deh men dem, if yu follow dem
Woman become nervous wreck.

CHRISTINE DONALD, Canada

GOOD OLD BODY

All those years:
where I didn't have boyfriends and that was OK
because I was fat so that was why;
where I did love women but it wasn't physical
because fat women don't have sexual feelings

so I wasn't – you know – no;
those years of the many love poems
with no gender-betraying pronouns,
no corporeal substance – and no punishment following;
those times made safely possible by being fat.

And now the news:
women who love women
are allowed to cherish their bodies
as they are (if they want to).

■■ **CHARMAINE CROWELL, USA**

FAT BLUES

So you're twenty-five, three kids, on welfare and getting fat.
You go to night clubs, to hear musicians play, hoping you get
    a play.
        Drink singapore slings and get fat.

He say 'can we', you say 'I might as well'
he might be prince charming taking me out of hell

              So you take your pill and get fatter.
                You wine him and dine him and
                    constantly remind him
                    of all the lovely, and great

    you eat a little more and drink a little more

    Say he beginning to stay out late.

forget about him! think about yourself and
with that you will never lose
and you will never have to sing
that song with the old familiar ring called . . .

the fat blues.

■■ CHRISTINE DONALD, Canada

Poem untitled

The thin women woo each other
with phrases from books and old letters,
setting torch to the blue
touchpaper of familiar expectation,
flaring up with a fifty per cent mixture
of hot air and pure fuel.

Insecure in courtship,
inarticulate in love,
the fat woman's emotions lag behind
both her dreams and her realities,

fearful to lay claim
to the thin conventions of romance,
afraid of bulging out
of the slinky dress of sex-on-fire.

■■ VALERIE BLOOM, Jamaica

WHA FE CALL I'

Miss Ivy, tell me supmn,
An mi wan' yuh ansa good.
When yuh eat roun 12 o'clock,
Wassit yuh call yuh food?

For fram mi come yah mi confuse,
An mi noh know which is right,
Weddah dinnah a de food yuh eat midday,
Or de one yuh eat a night.

Mi know sey breakfus a de mawnin one
But cyan tell ef suppa a six or t'ree,
An one ting mi wi nebba undastan,
Is when yuh hab yuh tea.

Miss A dung a London ha lunch 12 o'clock,
An dinnah she hab bout t'ree,
Suppa she hab bout six o'clock,
But she noh hab noh tea.

Den mi go a Cambridge todda day,
Wi hab dinnah roun' bout two,
T'ree hour later mi frien she sey,
Mi hungry, how bout yuh?

Joe sey im tink a suppa time,
An mi sey yes, mi agree,
She halla, 'Suppa? a five o'clock,
Missis yuh mussa mean tea!'

Den Sunday mi employer get up late,
Soh she noh hab breakfus nor lunch,
But mi hear she a talk bout 'Elevenses',
An one sinting dem call 'Brunch'.

Breakfus, elevenses, an brunch,
lunch, dinnah, suppa, tea,
Mi brain cyan wuk out which is which,
An when a de time fe hab i'.

For jus' when mi mek headway,
Sinting dreadful set mi back,
An dis when mi tink mi know dem all,
Mi hear bout one name snack.

Mi noh tink mi a badda wid no name,
Mi dis a nyam when time mi hungry,
For doah mi 'tomach wi glad fe de food,
I' couldn care less whey mi call i'.

THE DIET

Sat in the pub
Drink flowing free
Everyone's merry
Cept poor old me
I'm starving

I have to sit
in the corner
All quiet
The trouble you see
I'm on a diet
I'm starving

No whisky, no gin
Why did I come in
no ploughman's lunch
like that greedy bunch
I'm starving

Shall I walk to the bar
I won't go too far
Just a pkt of crisps
and one drink
I'm starving

Then I think I'll have
when I've finished this fag
some chicken and chips
in a basket
I'm starving

No I can't keep quiet
I'll shout, Bugger the diet
I'm absolutely starving

// GRACE NICHOLS, born 1950, Guyana

INVITATION

I
If my fat
was too much for me
I would have told you
I would have lost a stone
or two

I would have gone jogging
even when it was fogging
I would have weighed in
sitting the bathroom scale
with my tail tucked in

I would have dieted
more care than a diabetic

But as it is
I'm feeling fine
feel no need
to change my lines
when I move I'm target light

Come up and see me sometime

II
Come up and see me sometime
Come up and see me sometime

My breasts are huge exciting
amnions of watermelon
                              your hands can't cup
my thighs are twin seals
                              fat slick pups

there's a purple cherry
below the blues
                of my black seabelly
there's a mole that gets a ride
each time I shift the heritage
of my behind

Come up and see me sometime

 ANON.

WHISTLE, DAUGHTER, WHISTLE (SONG)

Mother, I long to get married
  I long to be a bride,
I long to lay by that young man
  And close to by his side
Close to by his side
  O happy I should be,
For I'm young and merry and almost weary
  Of my virginity.

O daughter, I was twenty
  Before that I was wed,
And many a long and lonesome mile
  I carried my maidenhead.
O mother, that may be
  But it's not the case by me,
For I'm young and merry and almost weary
  Of my virginity.

// BELLA AKHMADULINA, born 1937, USSR
(translated from Russian by Stephan Stepanchev)

THE BRIDE

Oh to be a bride
Brilliant in my curls
Under the white canopy
Of a modest veil!

How my hands tremble,
Bound by my icy rings!
The glasses gather, brimming
With red compliments.

At last the world says yes;
It wishes me roses and sons.
My friends stand shyly at the door,
Carrying love gifts.

Chemises in cellophane,
Plates, flowers, lace . . .
They kiss my cheeks, they marvel
I'm to be a wife.

Soon my white gown
Is stained with wine like blood;
I feel both lucky and poor
As I sit, listening, at the table.

Terror and desire
Loom in the forward hours.
My mother, the darling, weeps —
Mama is like the weather.

. . . My rich, royal attire
I lay aside on the bed.
I find I am afraid
To look at you, to kiss you.

Loudly the chairs are set
Against the wall, eternity . . .
My love, what more can happen
To you and to me?

◢◢ SAPPHO, sixth century BC, Greece
(translated by Josephine Balmer)

Poem untitled

Lucky bridegroom,
the marriage you have prayed for has come to pass
and the bride you dreamed of is yours . . .

Beautiful bride,
to look at you gives joy; your eyes are like honey,
love flows over your gentle face . . .

Aphrodite
has honoured you above all others

◢◢ CHRISTINE CRAIG, Jamaica

POEM FOR A MARRIAGE

My love I learned
to trim the branches
of my fears for you.
Now I sense you lifting
slightly your protective shell
for me.

It was such a glorious, shapely shell,
comforting, cool inside.
But even when the day is harsh
I love the sun. I will bare
my face, throw wide my arms
and love you more on the open plain.

▟▟ LADY ANNE LINDSAY, 1750–1825, Britain

AULD ROBIN GRAY

When the sheep are in the fauld, and the kye at hame
And a' the warld to rest are gane,
The waes o'my heart fa' in showers frae my e'e,
While my gudeman lies close to me.

Young Jamie lo'ed me weel, and sought me for his bride;
But saving a croun he had naething else beside:
To make the croun a pund, young Jamie gaed to sea;
And the croun and the pund were baith for me.

He hadna been awa' a week but only twa,
When my father brak his arm, and the cow was stown awa';
My mother she fell sick, – and my Jamie at the sea –
And auld Robin Gray came a-courtin' me.

My father couldna work, and my mother couldna spin;
I toiled day and night, but their bread I couldna win;
Auld Rob maintained them baith, and wi' tears in his e'e
Said, 'Jennie, for their sakes, O marry me.'

My heart it said nay; I looked for Jamie back;
But the wind it blew high, and the ship it was a wrack;
His ship it was a wrack – Why didna Jamie dee?
Or why do I live to cry, Wae's me!

My father urged me sair: my mother didna speak;
But she look'd in my face till my heart was like to break:
They gi'ed him my hand, tho my heart was in the sea;
Sae auld Robin Gray he was gudeman to me.

I hadna been a wife a week but only four,
When mournfu' as I sat on the stane at the door,
I saw my Jamie's wraith – for I couldna think it he,
Till he said, 'I'm come hame to marry thee.'

O sair, sair did we greet, and muckle did we say;
We took but ae kiss, and tore ourselves away:
I wish that I were dead, but I'm no like to dee;
And why was I born to say, Wae's me!

I gang like a ghaist, and I carena to spin;
I daurna think on Jamie, for that wad be a sin;
But I'll do my best a gude wife aye to be,
For auld Robin Gray he is kind to me.

⁄⁄ ÉVA TÓTH, born 1943, Hungary
(translated by Laura Schiff)

THE CREATION OF THE WORLD

The first day
      I came to in the dark cold trembling
      while I gathered twigs lit them he came out
      of the cave shivered held his hands over
      the fire and said: Let there be light
The second day
      I woke at dawn carried water from the river
      to wet the clay ground so the dust wouldn't
      whip his face he came out I poured water into
      his palms he washed his face looked up and
      said: Let's call the sky roof the dryness earth
      and the gathered waters the seas
The third day
      I got up early picked blue red yellow fruit
      piling small seeds between two stones ground
      kneaded roast them he awoke stretched ate the
      bread the sweet fruit said: Let the earth
      bear tender grasses grasses with seeds fruit
      trees

The fourth day
            I awoke suddenly swept the yard with a branch
            of leaves soaked the laundry scrubbed the
            pots cleaned the tools he woke as I sharpened
            the scythe rolled over and said: Let heavenly
            bodies light the sky to divide day from night.
The fifth day
            I rode in the morning filled the troughs
            gave the horses hay milked the cows
            sheared the sheep grazed the goats stuffed
            the geese cut nettles for the ducklings
            ground corn for the hens cooked slops for
            the pigs threw the dog a bone poured the cat
            its milk he yawned slowly rubbed the sleep from his
            eyes and said: Let everything multiply and
            grow and cover the earth
The sixth day
            Pains woke me I gave birth to my child cleaned
            swaddled nursed him he leaned over let the
            little hand squeeze his thumb he smiled at
            his likeness and saw that truly all of his creation
            was good
The seventh day
            The baby's crying woke me I quickly changed
            his diapers nursed him he quieted down I
            lit the fire aired the apartment brought
            up the newspaper watered the plants dusted quietly
            made breakfast the smell of coffee woke him he turned
            on the radio lit a cigarette and blessed the seventh day

✌ ANNA WICKHAM, 1884–1947, UK

THE MARRIAGE

What a great battle you and I have fought!
A fight of sticks and whips and swords,
A one-armed combat,
For each held the left hand pressed close to the
    heart,
To save the caskets from assault.

How tenderly we guarded them;
I would keep mine and still have yours,
And you held fast to yours and coveted mine.
Could we have dropt the caskets
We would have thrown down weapons
And been at each other like apes,
Scratching, biting, hugging
In exasperation.

What a fight!
Thank God that I was strong as you,
And you, though not my master, were my match.
How we panted; we grew dizzy with rage.
We forgot everything but the fight and the love of
    the caskets.

These we called by great names –
Personality, Liberty, Individuality.

Each fought for right to keep himself a slave
And to redeem his fellow.
How can this be done?

But the fight ended.
For both was victory
For both there was defeat.
Through blood we saw the caskets on the floor.
Our jewels were revealed;
An ugly toad in mine,
While yours was filled with most contemptible
    small snakes:
One held my vanity, the other held your sloth.

The fight is over, and our eyes are clear. —
Good friend, shake hands.

// SILA (between 700 and 1050), India
(translated from Sanskrit by Willis Barnstone)

Poem untitled

My husband is the same man
who first pierced me.
We knew long evenings wet with the moon.
Wind from the hills of Vindhya
was heavy with fresh jasmine.
I am the same woman
yet I long for the stream and its reeds
which knew us happy. Which knew us
graceful
in endless evenings of making love.

// ELAINE FEINSTEIN, born 1930, UK

MARRIAGE

Is there ever a new beginning when every
word has its ten years' weight, can there be
what you call conversation between us?
Relentless you are as you push me
to dance and I lurch away from you
weeping, and yet can we bear to lie
silent under the ice together like
fish in a long winter?

A letter now from York is a reminder of
windless Rievaulx, the hillside moving through
limestone arches, in the ear's liquid the
whir of dove notes: we were a fellowship of three
strangers walking in northern brightness, our
searches peaceful, in our silence the
resonance of stones only, any celibate
could look for such retreat, for me
it was a luxury to be insisted on
in the sight of those grass-overgrown dormitories

We have taken our shape from the
damage we do one another, gently as
bodies moving together at night, we amend
our gestures, softly we hold our places:
in the alien school morning in the
small stones of your eyes I know how
you want to be rid of us, you were
never a family man, your virtue is
lost, even alikeness deceived us
love, our spirits sprawl together
and both at last are distorted

and yet we go toward birthdays and other
marks   not wryly   not thriftily
waiting, for where shall we find it, a
joyous, a various world? in fury
we share, which keeps us, without
resignation: tender whenever we touch   what
else we share   this flesh   we
bring together   it hurts to
think of dying as we lie close

▟▟ ANNA WICKHAM, 1884–1947, UK

NERVOUS PROSTRATION

I married a man of the Croydon class
When I was twenty-two.
And I vex him, and he bores me
Till we don't know what to do!
It isn't good form in the Croydon class
To say you love your wife,
So I spend my days with the tradesmen's books
And pray for the end of life.

In green fields are blossoming trees
And a golden wealth of gorse,
And young birds sing for joy of worms:
It's perfectly clear, of course,
That it wouldn't be taste in the Croydon class
To sing over dinner or tea:
But I sometimes wish the gentleman
Would turn and talk to me!

But every man of the Croydon class
Lives in terror of joy and speech.
'Words are betrayers', 'Joys are brief' —
The maxims their wise ones teach —
And for all my labour of love and life
I shall be clothed and fed,
And they'll give me an orderly funeral
When I'm still enough to be dead.

I married a man of the Croydon class
When I was twenty-two.
And I vex him, and he bores me
Till we don't know what to do!
And as I sit in his ordered house,
I feel I must sob or shriek,
To force a man of the Croydon class
To live, or to love, or to speak!

⫽ SUMANGALA'S MOTHER
(translated from Pali by Willis Barnstone)

Poem untitled

A free woman. At last free!
Free from slavery in the kitchen
where I walked back and forth stained
and squalid among cooking pots.
My brutal husband ranked me lower
than the shade he sat in.
Purged of anger and the body's hunger,
I live in meditation
in my own shade from a broad tree.
I am at ease.

// ANON., Canada
(translated by Carl Cary)

DIVORCE SONG OF BRITISH COLUMBIA NATIVE TRIBE

I thought you were good.
I thought you were like silver;
You are lead.

You see me high up on the mountain.
I walk through the sun;
I am sunlight myself.

// MAYA ANGELOU, born 1928, USA

THEY WENT HOME

They went home and told their wives,
    that never once in all their lives,
    had they known a girl like me,
But . . . They went home.

They said my house was licking clean,
    no word I spoke was ever mean,
    I had an air of mystery,
But . . . They went home.

My praises were on all men's lips
    they liked my smile, my wit, my hips,
    they'd spend one night, or two or three,
But . . .

III LADY ISE, 875?–938?, Japan
(translated by Etsuko Terasaki and Irma Brandeis)

Poem untitled

Because we suspected
the pillow would say 'I know',
we slept without it.
Nevertheless my name
is being bandied like dust.

III ROSEMARY TONKS, UK

STORY OF A HOTEL ROOM

THINKING we were safe – insanity!
We went to make love. All the same
Idiots to trust the little hotel bedroom.
Then in the gloom . . .
. . . And who does not know that pair of shutters
With the awkward hook on them
All screeching whispers? Very well then, in the gloom
We set about acquiring one another
Urgently! But on a temporary basis
Only as guests – just guests of one another's senses.

But idiots to feel so safe you hold back nothing
Because the bed of cold, electric linen
Happens to be illicit . . .
To make love as well as that is ruinous.
Londoner, Parisian, someone should have warned us
That without permanent intentions
You have absolutely no protection
– If the act is clean, authentic, sumptuous,
The concurring deep love of the heart
Follows the naked work, profoundly moved by it.

■■ DESANKA MAKSIMOVIC, born 1898, Yugoslavia
(translated from Croation by Vasa D. Mihailovich)

FOR ALL MARY MAGDALENES

I seek mercy
for the women stoned
and their accomplice – the darkness of the night,
for the scent of clover and the branches
on which they fell intoxicated
like quails and woodcocks,
for their scorned lives,
for their love torments,
unrelieved by compassion.
I seek mercy
for the moonlight and for the rubies,
of their skin,
for the moonlight's dusk,
for the showers of their undone hair,
for the handful of silvery branches,
for their loves naked
and damned –
for all Mary Magdalenes.

■■ JUDITH KAZANTZIS, born 1940, UK

IN MEMORY, 1978

I want to lament the princess who was killed,
gunned down by the henchmen of her grandfather,
        in the main square of Jeddah;
she was a princess so she was gunned,
ordinary women are stoned to death for adultery,
their lovers lose their heads, which is to
teach other men not to;

for the women the lorry reverses into the square,
        tips out a pile of ordinary stones
which at sunset are picked out by the faithful
under the adjuration of a holy man;
they being all men; the adulteress is made to
        stand upright inside a sack,
they throw stones at her till the sack falls
        over, and go on till she dies.

When the sun sets, here the crescent
rises — she sees neither,
having been a believer all her life, done
everything dutifully but one thing:
which was to remain behind her black seven veils
every living moment: to
take her flesh to sackcloth from birth
to death; to
keep their eyes clean
        for God, and his rigid kings and small fathers
on earth
        she salaams down
on to, dear God, well trodden ground.

// NURUNNESSA CHOUDHURY, born 1943, Bangladesh
(translated by Nurunnessa Choudhury and Paul Joseph Thompson)

DEATH OF A DOVE

In the first sunbath
of your love
my voice stole
the dawn bird's song.
On the horizon, I heard
the call of infinite life.
Then, the world was huge, I thought
the horizon would give way
to my child's flight

if we spread our wings
and flew side by side.
But now,
by the attraction of a forbidden fruit,
we are both prisoners — you and I.
The world has shrunk,
becoming a still life,
framed on a window sill.

In this picture is a lamp-post —
standing wanly like a miser's gift.
The sky is there too —
but wants to pull away
in frustration from
the damp walls.

You are very original!
After reading the newspaper
you are wonderfully original,
with news of a wide world
in the midst of
your unemployed friends and gamblers.
Now through the window I stare —
and see, coming,
with jealous and bloodshot eyes,
Poverty. And I fear
that he will take the bird of dawn —
the Dove, and
after plucking the feathers
of its imagination
will cast it into the fire.

// CHRISTINE DE PISAN, 1364–1430, France
(translated from French by Tom Vaughan)

BALLADE

Lone am I, and would be
Lone has my sweet love left me
Lone, without lord or friend
Lone, grieving and saddened
Lone, without ease I languish
Lone as a soul in anguish
Lone, since my love I lack

Lone am I, at door or casement
Lone, in this corner pent
Lone, on my tears feeding
Lone, whether calm or grieving
Lone, never so chagrined
Lone, in my closet confined
Lone, since my love I lack

Lone am I, wherever I stray
Lone, when I walk or stay
Lone, as none to earth's ends
Lone, abandoned by friends
Lone am I, never so low
Lone, as my tears flow
Lone, since my love I lack

Envoi:

Prince, my grief is only dawning
Lone am I, and overcome by mourning
Lonely I wait, in sombre grey not black
Lone, since my love I lack

GABRIELA MISTRAL, 1889–1957, Chile
(translated from Spanish by Muriel Kittel)

BALLAD

He went with another;
I have seen him go.
Ever fair was the wind
and the path full of peace.
My eyes, my poor eyes
have seen him go!

He is falling in love with another
upon the flowering earth.
The thorn bush is blooming;
a song goes floating by.
And he is falling in love with another
upon the flowering earth!

He has kissed the other
on the shores of the sea;
the orange blossom moon
was gliding over the waters.
And my blood did not anoint
the sea's expanse!

He will go away with the other
for all eternity.
There will be fair skies
(God wishes to keep still)
And he will go away with the other
for all eternity.

HUANG HO, 1498–1569, China
(translated by Kenneth Rexroth and Ling Chung)

TO THE TUNE 'THE FALL OF A LITTLE WILD GOOSE'

Once upon a time I was
Beautiful and seductive,
Wavering to and fro in
Our orchid scented bedroom.
You and me together tangled
In our incense filled gauze
Bed curtains. I trembled,
Held in your hands. You carried
Me in your heart wherever
You went. Suddenly
A bullet struck down the female
Mandarin duck. The music
Of the jade zither was forgotten.
The phoenixes were driven apart.

I sit alone in a room
Filled with Spring, and you are off,
Making love with someone else,
Happy as two fish in the water.

That insufferable little bitch
With her coy tricks!
She'd better not forget –
This old witch can still
Make a furious scene.

// NINA CASSIAN, born 1924, Romania
(translated by Laura Schiff)

LADY OF MIRACLES

Since you walked out on me
I'm getting lovelier by the hour.
I glow like a corpse in the dark.
No one sees how round and sharp
my eyes have grown
how my carcass looks like a glass urn,
how I hold up things in the rags of my hands,
the way I can stand though crippled by lust.
No, there's just your cruelty circling
my head like a bright rotting halo.

// MAHSATI, twelfth century, Iran
(translated from Farsi by Deirdre Lashgari)

SELECTED QUATRAINS

I knew like a song your vows weren't strong,
   I knew they'd soon be broken.
This cruelty you've shown me, my friend, this wrong,
   I knew before it was spoken.

Gone are the games we played all night,
   gone the pearls my lashes strung.
You were my comfort and my friend.
    You've left, with all the songs I'd sung.

WHAT'LL THE NEIGHBOURS SAY? (SONG)

Once I loved a sailor, who often enjoyed my charms,
Now he's gone away and left me with a baby in my arms
   But all I get from my mother the livelong night and day is
   'Now you'll never be married in white and what'll the
     neighbours say?'

But I'm happy as a queen if all the truth be told
I prefer his little boy to any band of gold
   So keep your dress and your wedding ring, I'm happy all the
     day
   As long as my baby's on my knee I don't care what the
     neighbours say.

// GENEVIEVE TAGGARD, 1894–1948, USA

WITH CHILD

Now I am slow and placid, fond of sun,
Like a sleek beast, or a worn one:
No slim and languid girl – not glad
With the windy trip I once had,
But velvet-footed, musing of my own,
Torpid, mellow, stupid as a stone.
You cleft me with your beauty's pulse, and now
Your pulse has taken body. Care not how
The old grace goes, how heavy I am grown,
Big with this loneliness, how you alone
Ponder our love. Touch my feet and feel
How earth tingles, teeming at my heel!
Earth's urge, not mine – my little death, not hers;
And the pure beauty yearns and stirs,
It does not heed our ecstasies, it turns
With secrets of its own, its own concerns,

Toward a windy world of its own, toward stark
And solitary places. In the dark,
Defiant even now, it tugs and moans
To be untangled from these mother's bones.

// YOSANO AKIKO, 1878–1942, Japan
(translated by Kenneth Rexroth and Ikuko Atsumi)

LABOUR PAINS

I am sick today,
sick in my body,
eyes wide open, silent,
I lie on the bed of childbirth.

Why do I,
so used to the nearness of death,
to pain and blood and screaming,
now uncontrollably tremble with dread?

A nice young doctor tried to comfort me,
and talked about the joy of giving birth.
Since I know better than he about this matter,
what good purpose can his prattle serve?

Knowledge is not reality.
Experience belongs to the past.
Let those who lack immediacy be silent.
Let observers be content to observe.

I am all alone,
totally, utterly, entirely on my own,
gnawing my lips, holding my body rigid,
waiting on inexorable fate.

There is only one truth.
I shall give birth to a child,
truth driving outward from my inwardness.
Neither good nor bad; real, no sham about it.

With the first labour pains,
suddenly the sun goes pale.
The indifferent world goes strangely calm.
I am alone.
It is alone I am.

⁄⁄ MAUREEN HAWKINS, UK

THE MIRACLE

Before you were conceived
          I wanted you
Before you were born
          I loved you
Before you were here an hour
          I would die for you
This is the miracle of life.
The pain, so great,
was more than the throbbing of your final journey
into my love
But part of a process
that came accompanied with
New Life
New Consciousness
New Understanding
New Wisdom
A bigger heart
To accommodate
New Love
At last Liberation
At last Freedom
How special, how valuable
How close to all things right
Nine months of worry and expectation
Brought more than imagination can conjure
Never really knew
Until . . .

I feel you coming
I am ready for you
I am ready for life
I am rejuvenated
I am Blessed
with the gift of life.

// **GRACE NICHOLS, born 1950, Guyana**

IN MY NAME

Heavy with child

belly
an arc
of black moon

I squat over
dry plantain leaves

and command the earth
to receive you

in my name
in my blood

to receive you
my curled bean

my tainted

perfect child

      my bastard fruit
      my seedling
      my sea grape
      my strange mulatto
      my little bloodling

Let the snake slipping in deep grass
be dumb before you

Let the centipede writhe and shrivel
in its tracks

Let the evil one strangle on his own tongue
even as he sets his eyes upon you

For with my blood
I've cleansed you
and with my tears
I've pooled the river Niger

now my sweet one it is for you to swim

▮▮ SUSAN WALLBANK, born 1943, UK

WOMAN INTO MAN

I who have bred only daughters
watch in astonishment
this birthing of a son

girl flesh from woman born
seems natural
the folding out of one from one

but what strange alchemy
creates a gender change
what plan of nature?

what sleight of hand
lets out this rope that leads
from woman into man?

I think that now I understand
the fall from paradise
the loss of God

little crying wombless thing
you've work to do before
you lie once more inside

and she who is his mother
she does not seem to mind
his differentness

but with a kind of wonder
she reaches out to wrap
his small male body to her breast

// KIM NAM JO, born 1927, Korea
(translated by Ko Won)

MY BABY HAS NO NAME YET

My baby has no name yet;
like a new-born chick or a puppy
my baby is not named yet.

What numberless texts I examined
at dawn and night and evening over again!
But not one character did I find
which is as lovely as the child.

Starry field of the sky,
or heap of pearls in the depth.
Where can the name be found, how can I?

My baby has no name yet;
like an unnamed bluebird or white flowers
from the farthest land for the first,
I have no name for this baby of ours.

▐▐ ELIZABETH JENNINGS, born 1926, UK

FOR A CHILD BORN DEAD

What ceremony can we fit
You into now? If you had come
Out of a warm and noisy room
To this, there'd be an opposite
For us to know you by. We could
Imagine you in lively mood.

And then look at the other side,
The mood drawn out of you, the breath
Defeated by the power of death.
But we have never seen you stride
Ambitiously the world we know.
You could not come and yet you go.

But there is nothing now to mar
Your clear refusal of our world.
Not in our memories can we mould
You or distort your character.
Then all our consolation is
That grief can be as pure as this.

▐▐ GABRIELA MISTRAL, 1889–1957, Chile
(translated by D. M. Pettinella)

SLEEP CLOSE TO ME

Fold of my flesh
I carried in my womb,
tender trembling flesh
sleep close to me!

The partridge sleeps in the wheat
listening to its heartbeat.
Let not my breath disturb you
sleep close to me!

Little tender grass
afraid to live,
don't move from my arms;
sleep close to me!

I have lost everything,
and tremble until I sleep.
Don't move from my breast;
sleep close to me!

▟▌ JUDITH KAZANTZIS, born 1940, UK

AT THE NATIONAL GALLERY

A flow of people looking.
The baby sucks at its mother's breasts.
One tucked away, one full, the
nipple a guava fruit – dark and ready.
The mother, sitting in the National Gallery
on a blackbuttoned seat, in
an unzipped anorak, the baby slung,
could be copying the
Madonna she herself gazes at and drinks in,
over the way: a limpid, tidy
countenance on the wall there, her own
small teat held neatly with a crystal
cherry ending for the Christ Child Jesus
to nibble, who blesses us all.

The Keeper finds the mother of the guava
breast, and with a flurried frowning jerking
– the public don't want to see that sort of thing here
– orders her to take herself off, and baby and
breast, and zip it in quick. The
baby stops and cries, furious. Eyes flow past.
The mother feeds it again, looking at the wall.

Wrap it up – the Keeper
sees the broad breast, giving food
under his hand, so near he could stroke the skin.
– D'you want to make an exhibition of yourself?
He pulls her. She backs to the wall.
The Madonna of the Guava
(hung near the much loved
Madonna of the Cherry) is a fine recently
acquired picture attributed to.
Experts have judged it lifelike, for example in the
bluish pores of the nipple outstretched to the
lips of the child, still crying. It
now hangs in the National Gallery
– streams of people –
as part of the permanent collection.

▟▟ TAHEREH SAFFARZADEH, twentieth century, Iran
(translated from Farsi by Deirdre Lashgari)

BIRTHPLACE

I have never seen the place where I was born

the place my mother
laid beneath a ceiling
her womb's cumbrous load –
The first tick-tockings of my small heart
still live in the chimney fittings
and in the crannies of the old bricks
and there still visible on the door and walls
is that look of shame,
my mother's look
at my father
and my grandfather

A choked voice murmured
'It's a girl'
The midwife trembled
unsure of her birthing fee
– and goodbye to the circumcision feast

The first visit I make to my birthplace
I'll peel from the walls
that shamed look of my mother
and there where the bold rhythm of my pulse began
I'll make confession:
my clear hands
bear no urge to clench and strike
Brawling drunk isn't my language
I take no pride in killing
Male supremacy
never fattened me at its table

∕∕ RAFAELA CHACÓN NARDI, born 1926, Cuba
(translated by Margaret Randall)

MOUNTAIN GIRL

There is so much blossom and naked dawn
so much country air in you
circling your small figure.
You take the yagruma leaf
the river gives up, her dark plate,
and make a fan.
Music of all the birds you know
the scent of hills,
the rain's profile.
You invented a doll like no other:
carving her from dreams in dark wood.
And you cradle her against your virgin breast
hold her and sing
as the breeze in branches,
little mother.

▟▟ PENELOPE SHUTTLE, born 1947, UK

THE FLOWER-PRESS

We bend over my old flower-press,
mother and young daughter,
you full of excitement and chatter,
me nervous as I open it
after its years of dust-gathering
on the shelf.
In here we discover
the fastened flowers,
the originals I remember placing
carefully between the sheets
of green blotting paper,
fragments to me now,
ghosts of flowers,
the pressure has been too great
for their lives to bear.
Dry, frail, faded,
each leaf, petal and frond;
I lay them one by one
on your own hand.
Gathered and preserved from the years
before you were born,
to me these flowers are flawed.
For me their place has been taken by you,
my own flower, ever-growing, changing.
Am I right to warn you of their imperfections?
Should I try to show you how lives may be grasped,
and like these flowers shut in, immobilized?
Or am I bringing you too soon word of corruption,
too much stillness?
No matter, for you are not listening.
With bright eyes you say,
'aren't they beautiful, can I press some too?'
Seeing only the beauty.
So like pure air reaching into areas
long since sealed off, now reclaimable,

you lead me forward without fear.
Deeper and deeper you draw me into life,
you make the dead come alive again
by sensing how even the shadow of a flower
may be perfect, and so suffice.

MWANA KUPONA MSHAM, 1810–60, East Africa
(translated from Swahili by J. W. T. Allen; adapted by Deirdre Lashgari)

FROM POEM TO HER DAUGHTER

Daughter, take this amulet
tie it with cord and caring
I'll make you a chain of coral and pearl
to glow on your neck. I'll dress you nobly.
A gold clasp too – fine, without flaw
to keep with you always.
When you bathe, sprinkle perfume, and weave your
      hair in braids.
String jasmine for the counterpane.
Wear your clothes like a bride,
for your feet anklets, bracelets for your arms . . .
Don't forget rosewater,
don't forget henna for the palms of your hands.

JUDITH KAZANTZIS, born 1940, UK

FOR MY DAUGHTER

Don't be in a hurry, Miranda . . .
the old mother, you know
remembers herself at your age,
sixteen is it, well I,
well you are too beautiful, time
to leave . . . ?

Don't be in a hurry, my
smouldering eye-liner.
Keep your mane twirled round you.

As for those well formed
fishnet calves
pedalling to school
out of black suede
fringed high-heeled ankle boots
– to display
or disown? But that's a difficulty
you've got taped. Oh
nobody whistles, you say
scornfully when I wonder.
Clearly, you measured the world?

You prowl the house
like a crusader's queen, black
eyebrowed. The crusader herself,
my mail-fisted beauty . . .
Well, on your way then:
more strategy than I had.
You make me
remember bad years, the
loss of Jerusalem.
Hurry, Miranda . . .

Wait wait.

// OTOMO NO SAKANOE, eighth century, Japan
(translated from Japanese by Geoffrey Bownas and Anthony Thwaite)

SENT FROM THE CAPITAL TO HER ELDER DAUGHTER

More than the gems
Locked away and treasured
In his comb-box
By the God of the Sea,
I prize you, my daughter.

But we are of this world
And such is its way!
Summoned by your man,
Obedient, you journeyed
To the far-off land of Koshi.
Since we parted,
Like a spreading vine
Your eyebrows, pencil-arched,
Like waves about to break,
Have flitted before my eyes,
Bobbing like tiny boats.
Such is my yearning for you
That this body, time-riddled,
May well not bear the strain.

Had I only known
My longing would be so great,
Like a clear mirror
I'd have looked on you –
Not missing a day,
Not even an hour.

// MARY DORCEY, born 1950, Eire

DAUGHTER

And you my daughter
who I will not know –
I feel in mine
your small, hot hand,
I see your green eyes
lighting already
with my mother's far away look,
and the kisses
that might have made you
from my lover's warm, dark lips
smiling from yours –
made for kisses.

My little daughter
what times we shall have —
what talks.
I would hold up the stars
to keep from burning you
quiet the sea
to keep from waking you.
I would eat you for breakfast
all your fat, buttery flesh
thighs and arms
toast and honey.

My little daughter
you will not have the chance
to jail me with your tenderness
grow high and lovely
from my shrinking hide.

We will not now
confront each other
barter, threaten, promise
we will not curse each other
win or lose
my darling
we have no time for that.

I will bequeath you
little —
some words
angry, loving, careful
set down to make a space for you.

I will leave you
flowers and flame
scorched earth, black water
blue skies, laughter
hungry children
women working, loving
fire and ice
bombs and books

I will leave you
my daughter
this whole wide world
that was not yet
wide enough
for me
to bear you into.

MARY MACKEY, USA

GRANDE JETÉE

some rhythms must remain unbroken

like a dancer in an
arabesque
some women cannot carry
a child
in their arms

some come to salvation
drawn by the hands of small children

some can only make their leaps

alone.

CLARA ANN THOMPSON, nineteenth century, USA

MRS JOHNSON OBJECTS

Come right in this house, Will Johnson!
   Kin I teach you dignity?
Chasin' aft' them po' white children,
   Jest because you wan' to play.

Whut does po' white trash keer fah you?
    Want you keep away fum them,
Next, they'll be a-doing meanness,
    An' a-givin' you the blame.

Don't come mumblin' 'bout their playthings,
    Yourn is good enough fah you:
'Twas the best that I could git you,
    An' you've got to make them do.

Go'n' to break you fum that habit,
    Yes, I am! An' mighty soon,
Next, you'll grow up like the white-folks,
    All time whinin' fah the moon.

Runnin' with them po' white children –
    Go'n' to break it up, I say! –
Pickin' up their triflin' habits,
    Soon, you'll be as spilte as they.

Come on here, an' take the baby –
    Mind now! Don't you let her fall –
'Fo' I'll have you runnin' with them,
    I won't let you play at all.

Jest set there, an' mind the baby
    Till I tell you – You may go;
An' jest let me ketch you chasin'
    Aft' them white trash any mo'.

// MOIRA O'NEILL, 1864–1955, Ireland

HER SISTER

'Brigid is a Caution, sure,' – What's that ye say?
Is it my sister then, Brigid MacIlray?
Caution or no Caution, listen what I'm tellin' ye . . .
Childer, hould yer noise there, faix; there's no quellin' ye . . .
Och, well, I've said it now this many a long day,
'Tis the quare pity o' Brigid MacIlray.

An' she that was the beauty, an' never married yet;
An' fifty years gone over her, but do ye think she'll fret?
Sorra one o' Brigid then, that's not the sort of her,
Ne'er a hate would she care though not a man had thought of
    her.
Heaps o' men she might a' had . . . Here, get out o' that,
Mick, ye rogue; desthroyin' o' the poor ould cat.

Ah, no use o' talkin'! Sure a woman's born to wed,
An' not go wastin' all her life by waitin' till she's dead.
Haven't we the men to mind, that couldn't for the lives o'
    them
Keep their right end uppermost, only for the wives o' them? –
Stick to yer pipe, Tim, an' give me to talk now!
There's the door fore'nenst ye, man; out ye can walk now.

Brigid, poor Brigid will never have a child,
An' she you'd think a mother born, so gentle an' so mild . . .
Danny, is it puttin' little Biddy's eyes out ye're after,
Swishin' wid yer rod there, an' splittin' wid yer laughter?
Come along the whole o' yez, in out o' the wet,
Or may I never but ye'll soon see what ye'll get.

She to have no man at all. . . . Musha, look at Tim!
Off an' up the road he is, an' wet enough to swim,
An' his tea sittin' waitin' on him, there he'll sthreel about now –
Amn't I the heart-scalded woman out an' out now?
Here I've lived an' wrought for him all the ways I can,
But the Goodness grant me patience, for I'd need it wid that man!

What was I sayin' then? Brigid lives her lone,
Ne'er a one about the house, quiet as a stone . . .
Lave a-go the pig's tail, boys, an' quet the squealin' now . . .
Mind; I've got a sally switch that only wants the peelin'
    now . . .
Ah, just to think of her, 'deed an' well-a-day!
'Tis the quare pity o' Brigid McIlray.

▟▌ PENELOPE SHUTTLE, born 1947, UK

MOTHER AND CHILD

My heart sharpened to a point
and piercing you,
my child,
who came when I called,
in the moonlight, years past,
in the little bedroom,
in the whiteness of the full moon –
I knew your sex, your name:
the prophesying was easy.
Time has brought us onward,
in its own sweet and hard way.

And my anger pierces you,
and transfixed, you watch me,
on your guard –
I pull back my weapon,
my sharpened heart pierces itself
and frees you,
and you bound away,
singing one of your own wild unique songs.

▟▌ ANNA WICKHAM, 1884–1947, UK

THE BOY AND THE DREAM

I thought of the delicate things he had said,
And, ruthless marauder, I went to his bed:
'You'll be a poet one day, maybe,
I'm hoping a far better poet than me.'
With a catch in the throat the thing was done,
I had thrown my load to my slip of a son.
He thrilled, and sat bolt up in his bed,
'Will you *really* buy me those soldiers?' he said.

// DENISE LEVERTOV, born 1923, USA

THE SUN GOING DOWN UPON OUR WRATH

You who are so beautiful —
your deep and childish faces,
your tall bodies —

Shall I warn you?

Do you know
what is was to have
a certitude of grasses waving
upon the earth though all
humankind were dust?
Of dust returning
to fruitful dust?

Do you already know
what hope is fading from us
and pay no heed,
see the detested grave-worm shrivel,
the once-despised,
and not need it?

Is there an odyssey
your feet pull you towards
away from now to walk
the waters, the fallen
orchard stars?
            It seems
your fears are only the old fears, antique
anxieties, how graceful;
they lay as cloaks on shoulders
of men long dead,
skirts of sorrow wrapped
over the thighs of legendary women.

Can you be warned?

If you are warned will your beauty
scale off, to leave
gaping meat livid with revulsion?

No, who can believe it.
Even I in whose heart
stones rattle, rise each day
to work and imagine.

Get wisdom, get understanding, saith
the ancient. But he believed
there is nothing new under the sun,
his future
rolled away in great coils forever
into the generations.
Among conies the grass
grew again
and among bones.
And the bones would rise.

If there is time to warn you,
if you believed there shall be
never again a green blade in the crevice,
luminous eyes in rockshadow:
if you were warned and believed
the warning,

would your beauty
break into spears of fire,

fire to turn fire, a wall
of refusal, could there be
a reversal I cannot

hoist myself high enough
to see,
plunge myself deep enough
to know?

NAGASE KIYOKO, born 1906, Japan
(translated by Kenneth Rexroth and Ikuko Atsumi)

MOTHER

I am always aware of my mother,
ominous, threatening,
a pain in the depths of my consciousness.
My mother is like a shell,
so easily broken.
Yet the fact that I was born
bearing my mother's shadow
cannot be changed.
She is like a cherished, bitter dream
my nerves cannot forget
even after I awake.
She prevents all freedom of movement.
If I move she quickly breaks,
and the splinters stab me.

KATHERINE GALLAGHER, born 1935, Australia

DISTANCES

I see my mother waving – her unfussed, smiling
au revoir, alone on her verandah,
a small figure half-covered by shadow.

I hold her wave, see myself sharing it
eightfold, once for each of us – a wave
we have grown into

as she perfected it, voiced it over years
listening for the two who died,
losses she carried into her skin,
her children
the only trophies she ever wanted.

Now I search her face
contained, real as light,
hear over her words sewn into
the wave, 'There are many kinds of love
and I have lived some of them.'

NANCY MOREJÓN, born 1944, Cuba
(translated by Kathleen Weaver)

MOTHER

My mother had no patio garden
but rocky islands
floating in delicate corals
under the sun.
Her eyes mirrored no clear-edged branch
but countless garrottes.
What days, those days when she ran barefoot
over the whitewash of orphanages,
and didn't laugh
or even see the horizon.
She had no ivory-inlaid bedroom,
no drawing-room with wicker chairs,
and none of that hushed tropical stained-glass.
My mother had the handkerchief and the song
to cradle my body's deepest faith,
and hold her head high,
banished queen —
She gave us her hands, like precious stones,
before the cold remains of the enemy.

TRYING ON FOR SIZE

Capsized on the bed
you roll
cane white legs
tapping the air.
You are pulling on your stockings
easier now this way
than to stand upright and bend.
You are laughing
because I've caught you at it
one of your secret stratagems.

On the beach in summer
years ago,
a birth mark on your calf
shamed you –
when you were young in summer
your limbs long and full
your shoulders broad.
You swam with mighty strokes
out so far
I watched in awe
until your beauty
was a bird or buoy
dancing between waves.

With each new day behind you
you ask
do you remember when
and I do, almost all of it
and more.

You were not always good.
You threatened with a wooden spoon
cursed me when there was no one else to curse.
At sea in your kitchen
you did not counsel or console,
you turned your eyes from trouble
having known too much of it
uncomforted yourself.

Going down the stairs now
behind your anxious, baby steps
I want to pick you up and carry you
or launch you down the banister
as you did me
in this house
when we were children together.

But you must take every step first
along this passage
we daughters follow after
each one of us
moving into the space
cleared by our mothers.

And with what fine nerve
what unthanked bravery
you confront this last world
you will discover before me.

I see your shy, jaunty smile
at the mirror —
see you say
what do you think?
As if death
were a foolish, extravagant hat
you were trying on for size.

ELAINE FEINSTEIN, born 1930, UK

DAD

Your old hat hurts me, and those black
    fat raisins you liked to press into
my palm from your soft heavy hand:
    I see you staggering back up the path
with sacks of potatoes from some local farm,
    fresh eggs, flowers. Every day I grieve

for your great heart broken and you gone.
    You loved to watch the trees. This year
you did not see their Spring.
    The sky was freezing over the fen
as on that somewhere secretly appointed day
    you beached: cold, white-faced, shivering.

What happened, old bull, my loyal
    hoarse-voiced warrior? The hammer
blow that stopped you in your track
    and brought you to a hospital monitor
could not destroy your courage,
    to the end you were
uncowed and unconcerned with pleasing anyone.

I think of you now as once again safely
    at my mother's side, the earth as
chosen as a bed, and feel most sorrow for
    all that was gentle in
my childhood buried there
    already forfeit, now for ever lost.

// DINAH BUTLER, born 1960, UK

TO MY FATHER

you
black man
made me raw umber
abandoned my mother
dead you claim me
for your lineage and I
rage a friction
to stay warm in my mother's
cool cramped land where
care bent gentle towards me
and flesh was split
I owe you less than minus
stand fire eyed and innocent
no stepping slow reverent
around the stone thrones of
peerless ancestors
still my curiosity
trails your blackness
you head the column
my life
I hover a question
should I bring you fine children
and tears crusting salt tracks
or the anger of a stale betrayal to
keep you on the cold side of a shuttered moment
for I cannot hide
in luscious Nigeria imagined
tied to a wishworld by your
bequest of confusion

JEAN LIPKIN, born 1926, South Africa

FATHER

Lately his haunch has grown stiff,
He cannot shift out of his own bent.
The silencer is off his chest.
Wheezing in the acoustic ear
He crackles with static.
His memory veers unchecked
And swerves into old times and places.
Grant to him his fraudulent boast;
In the host of this withering
Let him shiver with pleasure
Recalling the measure of youth's arena.
His tall story is now his truth.
Do not doubt his world however spacious,
For it is so, when men go down steeply
The sky grows big
The sky grows big.

MARGARET RECKORD, Jamaica

THE JOURNEY

Moon-soaked
she emitted
a cold radiance
that made all
who loved her
leave her alone

As well
they might —
hers was the single
silver track
upmountain
to the moon.

// **DINAH BUTLER, born 1960, UK**

ONE LIFE

When their vigilance slipped,
A woman would excel and fly free.
Some would fall back.
She simmers long after,
For ever potential.

She left us an afternoon,
A smiling gleam that
Spears piled decades.
She left silently in a pause
That was musty and heavy,
Her voice a ringing,
For ever fresh,
For ever scented.
She haunts.

The last days of suffering
Were off the edge
Of reckoning.
She was castled up.
We would not know her secret greyness.

The promontory she walked
Was delicate nosed,
Took all her energy
For concentration.
Skies reeled by,
Always she was absorbed in her precarious
Stepping
Until she was a bumpy stream
Fast running over stone,
Clear and claiming nothing for recognition.

Her enigma was not endearing.
No one loved her pride.
She had no well-chased style.
Such was the subtlety
With which she escaped comprehension
And so flew.

SUNITI NAMJOSHI, born 1941, India

CYTHERA

Small rivulets ran about her feet
  and backwards to the ocean.
I knew who she was,
  but she walked through the waves
and sat down beside me.
              I stayed very still.
She said that it was hot.
I didn't say anything, but I thought
  to myself I would make a poem
  out of this, of how I sat on a beach
  and gossiped with a goddess, and of
  how kind she was and friendly.
Her movements were slow. 'She's lazy,'
  I decided. 'Olympians have the time
  and are therefore unhurried.'
I wondered how I looked, but she was
  combing her hair. I waited quietly.
  And then she smiled. I was
  very ashamed. She was my friend
  and I had made her a goddess:
              that shamed me.

▟▟ SAPPHO, sixth century BC, Greece
(translated by Josephine Balmer)

Poem untitled

Immortal Aphrodite, on your patterned throne,
daughter of Zeus, guile-weaver,
I beg you, goddess, don't subjugate my heart
with anguish, with grief

but come here to me now, if ever in the past
you have heard my distant pleas
and listened; leaving your father's golden house
you came to me then

with your chariot yoked; beautiful swift sparrows
brought you around the dark earth
with a whirl of wings, beating fast, from heaven
down through the mid-air

to reach me quickly; then you, my sacred goddess,
your immortal face smiling,
asked me what had gone wrong this time and this time
why was I begging

and what in my demented heart, I wanted most:
'Who shall I persuade this time
to take you back, yet once again, to her love;
who wrongs you, Sappho?

For if she runs away, soon she shall run after,
if she shuns gifts, she shall give,
if she does not love you, soon she shall even
against her own will.'

So come to me now, free me from this aching pain,
fulfil everything that
my heart desires to be fulfilled: you, yes you,
will be my ally.

▟▟ CAROLE E. GREGORY, born 1945, USA

LOVE LETTER

Dear Samson,
I put your hair
in a jar
by the pear tree
near the well.
I been thinkin'
over what I done
and I still don't think
God gave you
all that strength
for you to kill
my people.

Love – Delilah

▟▟ MICHELENE WANDOR, UK

LILITH RE-TELLS ESTHER'S STORY

the world rustles for Esther
in her best red weave

only nine chapters, she has
little time to coin a magic mine

meanwhile, back at the palace, King Ahasuerus
feasts the men, while meanwhile
behind the palace, Queen Vashti
feasts the women.

Vashti is summoned to the king's presence
but being rosy with the jokes
of women, she puts her foot down

fuck off, you wally (or some Old Testament
equivalent), I won't be shown off like
a prize cow this time

the lads, of course, don't take to that at all
because everyone knows that once a queen
sets a bad eg
any woman could take it into her
head to disobey
her lord and master

get rid of Vashti, advise
the princes, fear seaming their pores,
replace her with another – after all,
every man
should bear rule
in his own house

so King A orders a load
of virgins (what's so special
about virgins?) from whom
to choose a replacement
for Vashti

meanwhile, back in the ghetto
Mordecai, the Jew, hears of this and sends
his cousin Hadassah (Esther to you)
along with the other virgins, and lo,
she is chosen with a select few
for further tests (the king conveniently
unaware of her ethnic origins)

a year of 'purification'; oil of
myrrh, sweet odours, and one by one,
in turn, in turn, the young women
are set before the king
for him to try
till he gets bored

Esther, however, does not bore him
at all, and as her reward, King A
sets the crown upon her head
and her body in his bed

Mordecai meanwhile hovers round the gate

also meanwhile, a bad man
called Haman
becomes King A's right-hand man,
a misnomer for such a sinister man
who likes all
to bow down
before him

Mordecai, always a meanwhile man,
refuses to bow, and in revenge Haman
decides to kill all
the Jews (where
have we heard that one since?)

anyway, the long and the short of it is that
Esther so continues to please King A
with her courage and her beauty
that Haman is sussed out
and hanged
the Jews are saved
and Mordecai rises
to be second-in-command
to King A

there is something missing
from this story:
someone
somewhere
doesn't bother to say
whether Esther
actually liked
King A

// FRANCES E. W. HARPER, 1825–1911, USA

VASHTI

She leaned her head upon her hand
    And heard the King's decree –
'My lords are feasting in my halls;
    Bid Vashti come to me.

'I've shown the treasures of my house,
    My costly jewels rare,
But with the glory of her eyes
    No rubies can compare.

'Adorned and crowned, I'd have her come,
    With all her queenly grace
And mid my lords and mighty men
    Unveil her lovely face.

'Each gem that sparkles in my crown,
    Or glitters on my throne,
Grows poor and pale when she appears,
    My beautiful, my own!'

All waiting stood the chamberlains
    To hear the Queen's reply.
They saw her cheek grow deathly pale,
    But light flashed to her eye:

'Go, tell the King,' she proudly said,
    'That I am Persia's Queen,
And by his crowd of merry men
    I never will be seen.

'I'll take the crown from off my head,
    And tread it 'neath my feet,
Before their rude and careless gaze
    My shrinking eyes shall meet.

'A Queen unveiled before the crowd!
    Upon each lip my name! –
Why, Persia's women all would blush
    And weep for Vashti's shame.

'Go back!' she cried, and waved her hand,
    And grief was in her eye:
'Go tell the King,' she sadly said,
    'That I would rather die.'

They brought her message to the King;
    Dark flashed his angry eye;
'Twas as the lightning ere the storm
    Hath swept in fury by.

Then bitterly outspoke the King,
    Through purple lips of wrath —
'What shall be done to her who dares
    To cross your monarch's path?'

Then spake his wily counsellors —
    'O, King of this fair land,
From distant Ind to Ethiop,
    All bow to thy command.

'But if, before thy servants' eyes,
    This thing they plainly see,
That Vashti doth not heed thy will
    Nor yield herself to thee.

'The women, restive 'neath our rule,
    Would learn to scorn our name,
And from her deed to us would come
    Reproach and burning shame.

'Then, gracious King, sign with thy hand
    This stern but just decree,
That Vashti lay aside her crown,
    Thy Queen no more to be.'

She heard again the King's command,
    And left her high estate;
Strong in her earnest womanhood,
    She calmly met her fate,

And left the palace of the King,
    Proud of her spotless name —
A woman who could bend to grief
    But would not bend to shame.

GILLIAN E. HANSCOMBE, born 1945, Australia

FROM JEZEBEL HER PROGRESS

1
Men made myths
and their mnemonic,
morality.
After that,
they passed judgments.

Therefore,
Jezebel is a seducer
to fornication and sacrilege.

Good, I thought, if
behind every man's fall
is a powerful woman.

I take you gladly, Jezebel;
the lift of your breasts, the
slide of your belly to thigh,
the rose of your chivalry.

But we must tell the daughters our intentions.

2
Tell me
come clean

Are you for Jesus king
or Jezebel queen?

Jesus king?
or Jezebel queen?

Do you think you don't choose either?
That both are neutered if you choose neither?

You liberals take care
You liberals beware:

Though you deny them
they still sit there

older than freedom of will.
Are you ready for the kill?

For lord's sake?
or lady's sake?

Are you ready for the kill?

3
Jolly Jezebel

jolly well done
jolly good girl

the swirl of crucifixes
in papal processions
makes you giggle
you ungodly girl
you witch
you bitch
seducer of men's souls

but women's souls?
that's another matter

Jesus Jezebel
I need a woman saviour

and I need a lover

let my cry come unto you
my heart have you
favour you with friends

4
Jesus and Jezebel
out of God's side or womb;
the one to glory gone
and then a tomb;

the other headed for a fall
and then a curse, without a hearse,
without a burial.

Jesus and Jezebel
heaven and hell
(light and dark

life and death

darlings of a
modern yin and yang)

leapt separately into the world.
Or so I'm told.

I'm not fooled.
Jezebel, my Jezebel, came first,
head first:
the seed of God still hot within her.

Jezebel
oh Jezebel.

// SUNITI NAMJOSHI, born 1941, India

LOOK, MEDUSA!

Medusa living on a remote shore
troubled no one: fish swam, birds flew, and the sea
did not turn to glass. All was as before.
A few broken statues lay untidily
on the lonely beach, but other than these
there was nothing wrong with that peaceful scene.
And so, when the hero, Perseus, came to seize
the Gorgon's head, he thought he might have been
mistaken. He watched for a while, but she turned
nothing to stone. The waves roared as waves will,
till at last the hidden hero burned
to be seen by her whom he had come to kill.
'Look, Medusa, I am Perseus!' he cried,
thus gaining recognition before he died.

✂✂ EUNICE DE SOUZA, India

REMEMBER MEDUSA?

My dumb ox loyalty is
the frozen heart
the frozen stare
of long aloneness
unpeopled even by terror

Remember Medusa,
who could not love
even herself?

Better the flailing
the angry words
burning through the brain
the certain sorrow

than letting go
than the fall
slow-motion
into that abyss

Each life-line of words
years in the making.

✂✂ MICHELENE WANDOR, UK

EVE MEETS MEDUSA

Medusa. Sit down. Take
the weight off your snakes. We have
a lot in common. Snakes, I mean.

Tell me, can you really turn men
to stone with a look? Do you
think, if I had a perm —
maybe not.

115

Don't you think
Perseus was
a bit of a coward? not even
to look you in the face

you were beautiful when you
were a moon goddess, before
Athene changed your looks
through jealousy

I can't see what's wrong
with making love
in a temple, even
if it was her temple

it's a good mask; you must
feel safe and loving
behind it

you must feel very powerful

tell me, what conditioner do you use?

// NURUNNESSA CHOUDHURY, born 1943, Bangladesh
(translated by Nurunnessa Choudhury and Paul Joseph Thompson)

I SEE CLEOPATRA

The working girl: child-carrying, sensual.
When I look at her, I see Cleopatra.
Cleopatra — my Cleopatra.
Your twin marriage
to immature children
made you a courtesan in the world's eyes.
Cleopatra — my Cleopatra:
You never had a house of your own,
never had shelter
in strong arms and chest,
deep like the jungle

where the baby deer can hide –
you only had
a suffering crown
of thorns – only a Queen,
by greedy and carnal Caesars
you were disrobed.

My unprotected Cleopatra –
the green god gave you love,
but could not give you shelter.
The refinement of your naked beauty
took away Mark Anthony's courage.

Loving Cleopatra: eternal mother:
Venus, Aphrodite: My Cleopatra!

Always like the cat
who delivers her own litter,
and carries her offspring in her mouth:
Every moment of your life spent in seeking shelter.

You sacrificed yourself proudly.
Your weapon was simply
The original and ultimate one:
And you were a solitary soldier.
Your pleasure ship, your
erotic movements were
your weapons of war.
The cry of victory in Octavius' wheels
will be extinguished, every time
he comes before your wound.
My Venus, Aphrodite, Cleopatra:
Your life was scandalous, dazzling: Undefeated!

CLEOPATRA

my body
she says
was roses once
and reeds from the Nile
my blood was resin wine
and my hair a skein
of black silk

I wanted to be
a pyramid once
standing alone in the desert
I wanted to be a fertile river
I wanted to be the moon

I wanted to stay
ten years old
forever
sink my roots in the mud
become a papyrus
make a scroll of myself
and never marry

when I was a girl
I was a hieroglyph
but now I'm a whore
to Caesar

now I dance topless
in a leopard skin
G string
Queen of the Nile
Priestess of Isis
twirling tassels
with silicone breasts
bigger than beach balls

never having any power
of my own
I've learned to seduce it

generals
emperors
business men
politicians
and professors
stand in line
to powder my ass

I wanted to be
a pyramid once
I wanted to be
the moon

now at night
sometimes
I feel
death
crawl towards me
on its belly

// ANNA AKHMATOVA, 1889–1966, USSR
(translated by D. M. Thomas)

CLEOPATRA

I am air and fire . . . Shakespeare

She has kissed lips already grown inhuman,
On her knees she has wept already before Augustus . . .
And her servants have betrayed her. Under the Roman
Eagle clamour the raucous trumpets, and the dusk has

Spread. And enter the last hostage to her glamour.
'He'll lead me, then, in triumph?' 'Madam, he will.
I know't.' Stately, he has the grace to stammer . . .
But the slope of her swan neck is tranquil still.

Tomorrow, her children . . . O, what small things rest
For her to do on earth – only to play
With this fool, and the black snake to her dark breast
Indifferently, like a parting kindness, lay.

▮▮ CHRISTINE CRAIG, Jamaica

THE CHAIN

I no longer care, keeping close my silence
has been a weight,
a lever pressing out my mind.
I want it told and said and printed down
the dry gullies,
circled through the muddy pools
outside my door.
I want it sung out high by thin-voiced elders,
front rowing murky churches.
I want it known by grey faces queuing under
greyer skies in countries waking
and sleeping with sleet and fog.
I want it known by hot faces pressed against
dust-streaked windows of country buses.

And you must know this now
I, me, I am a free black woman.
My grandmothers and their mothers
knew this and kept their silence
to compost up their strength,
kept it hidden
and played the game of deference
and agreement and pliant will.

It must be known now how that silent legacy
nourished and infused such a line,
such a close linked chain
to hold us until we could speak
until we could speak out
loud enough to hear ourselves
loud enough to hear ourselves
and believe our own words.

❚❚ MICHELLE T. CLINTON, USA

ANTI APART HATE ART

American blacks are known
for black magic & music &
humor, not black at all
but deep husky hearted
laughter that empties us
of hate.
Anti-hate we partay, we play,
make soul food easy
for white folks to swallow,
cut back on spice & the nasty
grease of history, nigguhs
be shame to be grouped
wit the jiga boos of the jungle,
beatin' drums, barefoot & ignorant.
Africa don't got the style
of new wave slick purple
pompadours, liberated negros
set the pace
in athletics, we the fastest,
hippest thang goin', doing the
well paid work of soothin' honkies
& stayin' high, hittin' the joint
to hide a shit colored memory of being
scum in this country, in this

world, being hung & strung out
in South Africa.

Happy negro. The news betrays your
joyous finger pop. (The white man ain't
done wit your ass yet.) The radio
reveals honkies' consistent cruelty
& america's indifference to lost
black blood. In Soweto, 32 killed,
20 something wounded in Sharpeville.
69 black pacifists made the street red.
The media conjures a hurting
that never touched my body
I grow out raged dread locks,
feed my babies greens,
sing 'em old blues & gospel,
I grow dread full black rage,
a tradition make me wish
for prison or guns but
america sweet assimilate,
off-white black culture
gotta make it soft
for whitie to comprehend
this evil possessing me,
gotta rise above
their stink like a saint,
be a Tutu, be a king,
anti apart hate
and spit out
an american black poem:
anti apart
hate
art.

▟▟ U. A. FANTHORPE, UK

YOU WILL BE HEARING FROM US SHORTLY

You feel adequate to the demands of this position?
What qualities do you feel you
Personally have to offer?

                                                    Ah

Let us consider your application form
Your qualifications, though impressive, are
Not, we must admit, precisely what
We had in mind. Would you care
To defend their relevance?

                                              Indeed

Now your age. Perhaps you feel able
To make your own comment about that,
Too? We are conscious ourselves
Of the need for a candidate with precisely
The right degree of immaturity.

                                      So glad we agree

And now a delicate matter: your looks.
You do appreciate this work involves
Contact with the actual public? Might they,
Perhaps, find your appearance
Disturbing?

                                            Quite so

And your accent. That is the way
You have always spoken, is it? What
Of your education? Were
You educated? We mean, of course,
Where were you educated?
                        And how
Much of a handicap is that to you,
Would you say?

                    Married, children,
We see. The usual dubious
Desire to perpetuate what had better
Not have happened at all. We do not
Ask what domestic disasters shimmer
Behind that vaguely unsuitable address.

And you were born –?

                                                    Yes. Pity

So glad we agree.

▮▮ MARSHA PRESCOD, UK

ANTI-RACIST PERSON

You're an anti-racist person,
concerned about my humble plight,
you want to help me get equality,
'cos I've had a disadvantaged life.

You believe we are multi-racial,
an dat I'm British, despite I'm black,
yet when I ask a question in de classroom,
is like yu nearly have a heart attack!

You're an anti-racist person,
you say everyone has equal start,
but when I go to you for job interview,
you look at me as if I fart.

You-like-to-watch-me-in-doc-u-*men*-tary,
set in far off place ona tv,
wearing loincloth, with native vices,
you feel concern about my crises,
but when I jump on me feet an move into your street,
yu screaming 'bout your property prices.

Yu study me in books an papers,
den yu talk to me above my head,
but while yu holding all yu fancy conf'rences,
your society is killing me dead.

You're an anti-racist person,
but excuse me if I must confess,
when I see your anti-racist policies,
I feel safer wid de real NF!

// **HIMANI BANNERJI, Pakistan, lives in Canada**

'PAKI GO HOME'

1
3 pm
sunless
winter sleeping in the womb of the afternoon
wondering how to say this
to reason or scream or cry or whisper
or write on the walls
reduced again
cut at the knees, hands chopped, eyes blinded
mouth stopped, voices lost.

fear anger contempt
thin filaments of ice and fire
wire the bodies
my own, of hers, of his,
the young and the old.

And a grenade explodes
in the body
in the sunless afternoon
and words run down
like frothy white spit
down her bent head
down the serene parting of her dark hair
as she stands too visible
from home to bus stop to home
raucous, hyena laughter,
'Paki, go home!'

2
The moon covers her face
pock-marked and anxious
in the withered fingers of the winter trees.
The light of her sadness runs like tears
down the concrete hills, tarmac rivers
and the gullies of the cities.
The wind still carries the secret chuckle.
The rustle of canes
as black brown bodies flee into the night
blanched by the salt waters of the moon.
Strange dark fruits on tropical trees
swing in the breeze gently.

3
Now, then and again
we must organize.
The woman wiping the slur spit
from her face, the child standing
at the edge of the playground silent, stopped.
The man twisted in despair,
disabled at the city gates.
Even the child in the womb
must find a voice
sound in unison
organize.
Like a song, like a roar
like a prophecy that changes the world.

To organize, to fight the slaver's dogs,
to find the hand, the foot, the tongue,
the body dismembered
organ by organ rejoined
organized.
Soul breathed in
until she, he
the young, the old is whole.
Until the hand acts moved by the mind
and the walls, the prisons, the chains of lead or gold,
tear, crumble, wither into dust
and the dead bury the dead
until yesterdays never return.

// GRACE NICHOLS, born 1950, Guyana

HI DE BUCKRAS HI!

Vexation of mind
Vexation of eye
Vexation of spirit

Vexation of mind
Vexation of eye
Vexation of spirit

Look at the buckra woman
head in parasol floating
by white and pale
being helped from carriages
being lifted over ditches
floating by white and pale
not even looking
not even seeing
the pain and rage and black
despair

Vexation of mind
Vexation of eye
Vexation of spirit

Vexation of mind
Vexation of eye
Vexation of spirit

(Bursts into song)

O buckra woman she come over de sea
with she round blue eyes from she
cold countree

She walk straight, she head high
she too fenky
she better take care she don't turn
zombie

O buckra man him come over de sea
with him pluck-chicken skin
from him cold countree

Him palaver him a pray him a dress
fancee but suddenly so him turning
weak and dizzy

O buckra woman she come over de sea
with she round blue eyes from she cold
countree

She walk straight she head high
she too fenky
she better take care she don't
turn zombie

She better take care she don't
turn zombie

Hi de buckras hi
Hi de buckras hi
Hi de buckras hi
O Hi de buckras hi!

⁄⁄ SOJOURNER TRUTH, 1797–1883, USA
(adapted to poetry by Erlene Stetson)

AIN'T I A WOMAN?

That man over there say
   a woman needs to be helped into carriages
and lifted over ditches
   and to have the best place everywhere.
Nobody ever helped me into carriages
   or over mud puddles
     or gives me a best place . . .

And ain't I a woman?
   Look at me
Look at my arm!
   I have plowed and planted
and gathered into barns
   and no man could head me . . .
And ain't I a woman?
   I could work as much
and eat as much as a man –
   when I could get to it –
and bear the lash as well
   and ain't I a woman?
I have born 13 children
   and seen most all sold into slavery
and when I cried out a mother's grief
   none but Jesus heard me . . .
and ain't I a woman?
   that little man in black there say
a woman can't have as much rights as a man
   cause Christ wasn't a woman
Where did your Christ come from?
   From God and a woman!
Man had nothing to do with him!
   If the first woman God ever made
was strong enough to turn the world
   upside down, all alone

together women ought to be able to turn it
   rightside up again.

There is no exact copy of this speech given at the Women's Rights Convention
in Akron, Ohio, in 1852. The speech has been adapted to the poetic format by
Erlene Stetson from the copy found in Sojourner, God's Faithful Pilgrim *by*
Arthur Huff Fauset (Chapel Hill: University of North Carolina Press, 1938).
(From the anthology Black Sister.*)*

// MARGARET RECKORD, Jamaica

MISS GEETA

She made her crossing
wedged like a splinter
on the slaver

and, disembarked
walked straight to Troja
and took a bushbroom
to an already spotless yard

Cooked porridge
with cinnamon stick and mace
blew firecoal till
she billowed to smoke,
aged as quietly
as ashes

Shrunk childhigh
inside her eternal
osnaburg of patches
she padded out the farm
on heels, mapped
like her river-origins

Holidays,
a single tooth star
would smile out
from under her tiehead
and, lavishing grater-cake
and dawn-coloured guavas
she listened, incredulous,
to city children
and their prattle

And when
each day
had been husked clean,
squeezed for its milky goodness
scoured, riverstone dried,
broom-beaten and aired
like the coir mattress
shone clear
like the sweethome lamps,
then, this uncomplaining African
wipe-washing arms and legs
to starapple sheen
by the standpipe – repeated
her unvarying litany of leave taking
and descended the hill
drawing the nightcurtain
down
behind.

The children ran
to the quickstick.
Pink-powdered by blossoms,
they strained
to mark her exit

sure they saw her
swell slowly upwards, hunch
into towering bamboo
or, swirling round an endless cape
spangled with peenywallies
mount the air

One morning
walking to meet her
by the river
they found her rags
and frayed cotta
neatly folded
around
a star.

// NANCY MOREJÓN, born 1944, Cuba
(translated by Kathleen Weaver)

I LOVE MY MASTER

I love my master.
I gather brushwood to start his daily fire.
I love his blue eyes.
Gentle as a lamb,
I pour drops of honey for his ears.
I love his hands
that threw me down on a bed of grasses.
My master bites and subjugates.
He tells me secret tales while
I fan all his body,
running with wounds and bullet-pierced
from long days in the sun and plundering wars,
I love his roving pirate's feet
that have pillaged foreign lands.
I rub them with the softest powders
I could find, one morning,
coming from the tobacco fields.
He strummed his ornate guitar and
melodious couplets soared,
as though from Manrique's throat.
I longed to hear a marimbula sound.
I love his fine red mouth
that speaks words I can't understand

132

for the language I speak to him
still isn't his own.

And the silk of time is in shreds.
Overhearing the old black overseers
I learned how my lover
doled out whip-blows
in the vatroom of the sugar-mill,
as if it were a hell, that of the Lord God
they harped upon so much.

What's he going to say to me?
Why do I live in this hole not fit for a bat?
Why do I wait on him hand and foot?
Where does he go in his lavish coach
drawn by horses that are luckier than me?
My love for him is like the creeping weeds
that overrun the private food-plots of the slaves,
the only thing I can really call my own.

I curse

this muslin robe he has draped over my shoulders;
these vain laces he has pitilessly made me wear;
my household tasks in the afternoon where
no sunflowers grow;
this language so stubbornly hostile I can't spit it out
these stone breasts that can't give him suck,
this belly slashed by his age-old whip;
this damned heart.

I love my master but every night
When I cross the blossoming path to the canefield,
the secret place of our acts of love,
I see myself knife in hand,
flaying him like an innocent animal.

Bewitching drumbeats
now drown his cries, his sufferings.
The bells of the sugar-mill call . . .

GRACE NICHOLS, born 1950, Guyana

SKIN-TEETH

Not every skin-teeth
is a smile 'Massa'

if you see me smiling
when you pass

if you see me bending
when you ask

Know that I smile
know that I bend
only the better
to rise and strike
again.

FRANCES E. W. HARPER, 1825–1911, USA

SHE'S FREE!

How say that by law we may torture and chase
A woman whose crime is the hue of her face? –
With her step on the ice, and her arm on her child,
The danger was fearful, the pathway was wild . . .
But she's free! yes, free from the land where the slave,
From the hand of oppression, must rest in the grave;
Where bondage and blood, where scourges and chains,
Have placed on our banner indelible stains . . .
The bloodhounds have miss'd the scent of her way,
The hunter is rifled and foiled of his prey,
The cursing of men and clanking of chains
Make sounds of strange discord on Liberty's plains . . .
Oh! poverty, danger and death she can brave,
For the child of her love is no longer a slave.

MARGARET ATWOOD, born 1939, Canada

A WOMAN'S ISSUE

The woman in the spiked device
that locks around the waist and between
the legs, with holes in it like a tea strainer
is Exhibit A.

The woman in black with a net window
to see through and a four-inch
wooden peg jammed up
between her legs so she can't be raped
is Exhibit B.

Exhibit C is the young girl
dragged into the bush by the midwives
and made to sing while they scrape the flesh
from between her legs, then tie her thighs
till she scabs over and is called healed.
Now she can be married.
For each childbirth they'll cut her
open, then sew her up.
Men like tight women.
The ones that die are carefully buried.

The next exhibit lies flat on her back
while eighty men a night
move through her, ten an hour.
She looks at the ceiling, listens
to the door open and close.
A bell keeps ringing.
Nobody knows how she got here.

You'll notice that what they have in common
is between the legs. Is this
why wars are fought?
Enemy territory, no man's
land, to be entered furtively,
fenced, owned but never surely,
scene of these desperate forays
at midnight, captures

and sticky murders, doctors' rubber gloves
greasy with blood, flesh made inert, the surge
of your own uneasy power.

This is no museum.
Who invented the word *love*?

// TERESITA FERNÁNDEZ, born 1930, Cuba
(translated by Margaret Randall)

UGLY THINGS (A SONG)

In an old worn-out basin
I planted violets for you
and down by the river
with an empty seashell
I found you a firefly.
In a broken bottle
I kept a seashell for you
and coiled over that rusty fence
the coral snake flowered
just for you.
Cockroach wing
carried to the ant hill:
that's how I want them to take me
to the cemetery when I die.
Garbage dump, garbage dump
where nobody wants to look
but if the moon comes out
your tin cans will shine.
If you put a bit of love
into ugly things
you'll see that your sadness
will begin to change color.

// YOLANDA ULLOA, born 1948, Cuba
(translated by Margaret Randall)

ITA

Tania died
with the fever of the task still waiting.

Heavy with music
she walked towards death
and her heart

travelled the waters of the great river
to burn out later
in its course.

From bank to bank
you could hear her voice
crossing the river.

From the bush
a woman wearing a soldier's boots
back-pack and a submachine gun
comes up to death.

We know
she raised her arms
to reach the weapons and fire.
Vargas the assassin
pierced her lung.

In the waters of the great river
her body travelled
fugitive from all forgetting,
her city eyes.

Ita forever, grown,
become woman in the blue militia uniform.
Ita forever
in the mountains
from bank to bank
along the river.

*'Ita' was what Tamara Bunke, or Tania the Guerrilla, was called as a child.
She was a German-Argentine revolutionary. She was killed in Bolivia in 1967
while a member of Ernesto Che Guevara's internationalist army.*

// ANNA AKHMATOVA, 1889–1966, USSR
(translated by D. M. Thomas)

EPILOGUE (FROM REQUIEM)

I

There I learned how faces fall apart,
How fear looks out from under the eyelids,
How deep are the hieroglyphics
Cut by suffering on people's cheeks.
There I learned how silver can inherit
The black, the ash-blond, overnight,
The smiles that faded from the poor in spirit,
Terror's dry coughing sound.
And I pray not only for myself,
But also for all those who stood there
In bitter cold, or in the July heat,
Under that red blind prison-wall.

II

Again the hands of the clock are nearing
The unforgettable hour. I see, hear, touch

All of you: the cripple they had to support
Painfully to the end of the line; the moribund;

And the girl who would shake her beautiful head and
Say: 'I come here as if it were home.'

I should like to call you all by name,
But they have lost the lists . . .

I have woven for them a great shroud
Out of the poor words I overheard them speak.

I remember them always and everywhere,
And if they shut my tormented mouth,

Through which a hundred million of my people cry,
Let them remember me also . . .

And if ever in this country they should want
To build me a monument

I consent to that honour,
But only on condition that they

Erect it not on the sea-shore where I was born:
My last links there were broken long ago,

Nor by the stump in the Royal Gardens,
Where an inconsolable young shade is seeking me,

But here, where I stood for three hundred hours
And where they never, never opened the doors for me.

Lest in blessed death I should forget
The grinding scream of the Black Marias,

The hideous clanging gate, the old
Woman wailing like a wounded beast.

And may the melting snow drop like tears
From my motionless bronze eyelids,

And the prison pigeons coo above me
And the ships sail slowly down the Neva.

// KATHERINE GALLAGHER, born 1935, Australia

THE SURVIVOR
For Anna Ahkmatova, 1889–1966

A woman sits in a corner of sun
tracing a poem. Slowly
she is woven into it like the day
as smells of burning
carry her outside.

There, soldiers and jailers
are blocking the street,
books are being burnt –
thousands of words collapsing
in on each other. Suddenly
she sees her own fate,
her fellow-poet is taken
leaving her only silence.

She goes back to continue the poem:
it will go on for twenty years
islanded in her head
and Russia will remember her
as a lover
waiting for the ice-walls to break,
for her hermit's cry
to be carried like fire
from hand to hand.

IRINA RATUSHINSKAYA, born 1954, USSR
(translated by David McDuff)

I WILL LIVE AND SURVIVE

I will live and survive and be asked:
How they slammed my head against a trestle,
How I had to freeze at nights,
How my hair started to turn grey . . .
I will smile. And will crack some joke
And brush away the encroaching shadow.
And I will render homage to the dry September
That became my second birth.
And I'll be asked: 'Doesn't it hurt you to remember?'
Not being deceived by my outward flippancy.
But the former names will detonate in my memory –
Magnificent as old cannon.
And I will tell of the best people in all the earth,
The most tender, but also the most invincible,
How they said farewell, how they went to be tortured,
How they waited for letters from their loved ones.
And I'll be asked: what helped us to live
When there were neither letters nor any news – only walls,
And the cold of the cell, and the blather of official lies,
And the sickening promises made in exchange for betrayal.
And I will tell of the first beauty
I saw in captivity.
A frost-covered window! No doors, nor walls,
Nor cell-bars, nor the long-endured pain –
Only a blue radiance on a tiny pane of glass,
A cast pattern – none more beautiful could be dreamt!
The more clearly you looked, the more powerfully dawned
Those brigand forests, campfires and birds!
And how many times there was bitter cold weather
And how many windows sparkled after that one –
But never was it repeated,
That upheaval of rainbow ice!
And anyway, what good would it be to me now,
And what would be the pretext for that festival?

Such a gift can only be received once,
And once is probably enough.

▰▰ MARGARET RANDALL, born 1936, USA

UNDER ATTACK
For Marian

Listen. These voices are under attack.

Ismaela of the dark tobacco house. Grandma.
A maid her lifetime of winters, granddaughter
of slaves.
Straight to my eyes:
'My mama used to tell me, one of these days
the hens gonna shit upwards!
And I'd stare at those hens' asses, wondering
when will it happen?
When we pushed the big ones down
and pulled the little ones up!'

'For Mama, Papa, and Blackie' she wrote
on the poem she left to say goodbye.
Nicaragua, 1977.
Disappear
or be disappeared.
Dora Maria whose gaze
her mother always knew. She trembled
at her first delivery,
then took a city fearlessly.

Rain and the river rising. Catalina
chases her ducks
that stray.
'And my months,' she cries,
on the platform with poles. A house
to do over and over. 'My months
gone in the hospital at Iquitos

and the full moon
bringing a madness to my head.'
Her body is light against my touch.
A woman's voice, parting
such density of rain.

Xuan, my cold hand in hers,
evokes the barracks.
'Soldiers who were our brothers.
Night after night, village by village.'
Quang Tri, 1974.
Gunfire
replaced by quiet conversation.
The work of women.
Xuan's history, too, is under attack.

Dominga brings her memory down
from the needle trade, Don Pedro,
her own babies
dead from hunger.
'I want to tell you my story, leave it
to the young ones
so they'll know.'
We are rocking. We are laughing.
This woman who rescued the flag at Ponce
Puerto Rico, 1937.
Known by that act alone.
Until a book
carries her words. Her voice.

I bring you these women.
Listen.
They speak, but their lives
are under attack.

They too are denied adjustment of status
in the land of the free. In the home of the brave.

RITA BOUMI-PAPPAS, Greece
(translated by Eleni Fourtouni)

ARTEMIS

This road I'm taking is long and bright
and cold
walking it at dawn, barefoot . . .

In prison I prepared for this trip
Women on death row stayed up all night with me
they gave me a change of clean clothes
and perfumed soap
they sprinkled rose water on my hair
and when they waved goodbye
they promised that it wouldn't be long
before we met again
from the iron-barred windows
they shouted – wait for us

Where am I?
which way is Kilkis and our house?
which way is the blue lake of Thoirani
I saw for the first time on a school outing?
I don't know this place
but my blood will be spilled here –
like wine in a wedding –
You get your guns ready – yawning
(don't hold it against me for waking you so early)
I comb my hair for the last time

Go on! hurry, what are you waiting for?
you want to know my last wish?

I'm 19. I don't want to die.

GRACE NICHOLS, born 1950, Guyana

ALA

Face up
they hold her naked body
to the ground
arms and legs spread-eagle
each tie with rope to stake

then they coat her in sweet
molasses and call us out
to see . . . the rebel woman

who with a pin
stick the soft mould
of her own child's head

sending the little new-born
soul winging its way back
to Africa – free

they call us out to see
the fate for all us rebel
women

the slow and painful
picking away of the flesh
by red and pitiless ants

but while the ants feed
and the sun blind her with
his fury
we the women sing and weep
as we work

O Ala
Uzo is due to join you
to return to the pocket
of your womb

Permit her remains to be
laid to rest – for she has
died a painful death

O Ala
Mother who gives and receives
again in death
Gracious one
have sympathy
let her enter
let her rest

// RITA BOUMI-PAPPAS, Greece
(translated by Eleni Fourtouni)

KRINIO

Aim straight at my heart
it has served me well up to now.
to make it easy for you
I've sewn this black piece of cloth
right in the middle of my breasts.

I don't know what your fire will be like
– poor beardless soldiers – they've got you up
at dawn on my account
I've never held a gun – I don't know

I see your eyes wide open
– you can't help all this –
your hands want to touch me
before they pull the trigger – I understand

You probably still have the nicknames
of your boyhood
and who knows, we might've played together in the streets

Go on, spare me the morning frost
I'm almost naked
dress me in your fire
smile at me boys
cover my body with your gaze

I've never been covered by a lover
not even in dream . . .

// NILENE O. A. FOXWORTH, USA

BE STILL HEART

I wish I could rest my mind
On an empty plane that's nil.
Just float in space like a cloud
And tell my heart be still.
Be still – Be still heart!

I see flies trying to nest
In the bellybutton of a starving baby
And feast on the open wound
Of a little old blind lady.
I see sisters doing the best they can . . .
Washing all the dirty clothes by hand.
Most Black folk ain't never seen
The luxury known as washing machine.
Be still heart!

Mother's mother
And father's father
Cultivated so much land . . .
With free labor!
Cheap labor!
Hard! labor
Black folk could hardly stand . . .
Hot labor!
Cold labor!
Kill! labor.
Reagan-thatcher-bota-ism
So we still labor.
Be still heart!

Been christianized and baptized
Yet, ghetto dehumanized.
Been integrated and assimilated
Yet, grisly degenerated.
Be still heart! Be still!

For there's a new day a comin
De-o-masta gonna be runin
(To and fro)
But masta won't find nowhere to go.
Masta created too much sin.
Now masta can't hardly find a friend.
Be still heart! Be still!
For there's a new day a comin.

▟▟ WENDY POUSSARD, born 1943, Australia

GREENHAM WOMEN

Rugged up for winter snow
you have put your bodies
where your hearts are . . .
against the gates and
under the wheels of war.
Today the missiles came
to Greenham Common.
We saw it in the papers
and wept for you.
You are our elder sisters,
making the time kindly
to send us greeting as
you beat against the storm.
Like you we sit
on the doorstep of the world's end
and will not look away.
The people long to know
something is indestructible.
It may be only you.

NO WAR

There'll be no war
I tell myself, looking at the sky
above the downs.
Stars pierce the tree, without harm.
A cow coughs in the field, by the house.
People drive home
on the main road, puttering
under the stars.
The downs shine in the dark.
By morning, they'll wear frost, and breathe bitterly –
What sort of warmth
will break here, one of
these last years, of a hundred
begun in the continuous coffins –
What sort of gasp of aftermath
of the remarkable, grandiose, limited
order and peace, split,
arms, legs, ideals, finishing –
Ash sealing the surface,
not even such softness as blood
but down to a shadow.
I can't tell.
Except, suicide
should not be wiping and scrawling itself
against these stars, or over
these actors of the cold, languorous downs,
or people going home,
or animals in the field
by my house, in the particular night.

THE DAY I ONCE DREAMED

This is the day I first thought of
in my closed eyes,
deep in my eyes,
the day I first thought of;
with the sun strands weaving,
sun drops sparkling
in the high streams,
on the high seas –
the day I once dreamed.

This is the day I first saw
down in my mind,
deep in my brain,
the day I first saw;
with the wild gulls calling,
barley sheen swishing
in the high wind,
on the high hill –
the day I once dreamed.

This is the day I first heard
far in my head,
away out of sight,
the day I first heard;
with the streets all glittering,
coloured throng shimmering
in the bright lights,
under the lamps –
the day I once dreamed.

That was the day I then saw,
the day I then heard,
when I opened my eyes,
when I unblocked my ears;
the day I then knew
when I focused my mind,
the day I then knew;

with the huge cloud thundering,
thick sky asphyxiating
right overhead,
night overhead,
all over the land –
that was the day I then knew:
the terrible night,
the night of the Bomb,
the night of the doom.
That was the night I then knew –
the night of the end of the world.

▟▟ DEBORAH LEVY, UK

FLESH

If they massacre me . . .
These Nuclearics
Will they wear little missiles
Around their necks

Instead of a crucifix?

Will they say
I died for them

A Whole Planet died for them

And eat Hot Atomic Buns
For Easter?

Will they sing leukaemia'd litanies
Sip cancerous communions
Worship malignant madonnas?

Will they tell my grandma who
Plaiting history through my hair
Said Change IS possible girl –
Locate your heart and use it well

That the heart is a hard little button
Called Deterrent?

Will they pop my blisters like I pop corn?

And will all the mamas
With the poisoned ovaries

And all the dadas
With radio-active sperm

HUG

Their cataract babas
And give thanks?

Will they still feel democratic
When all their white cells

Eat up all their red cells
Thus
Ridding themselves of the communist menace?

// JAYNE CORTEZ, born 1936, USA

EVERYTHING IS WONDERFUL

Under the urination of astronauts
and the ejaculation of polluted sparrows
and the evacuation of acid brain matter
everything is wonderful
except for the invasion and occupation
of Grenada
except for the avalanche of blood coagulating
in El Salvador

except for the brutal apartheid system
raging in South Africa
except for the threat of intervention
in Nicaragua
except for the war of repression
in Namibia
except for Pinochet creaming again
this very day
from the killing floor of Allende and Neruda
except for that
and the torrential rainfall
of cluster bombs falling in Beirut
everything is everything
wonderful and wonderful

// WENDY POUSSARD, born 1943, Australia

WOMEN ON THE ROAD TO PINE GAP

Australia's best-kept dead-end road
leads through the desert
to a barbed wire fence.
Around the corner, past the gates,
inside a clutch of giant perspex balls,
space war computers
keep the deadly secrets
of another country.
A grid prevents the entry
of unauthorised cows
and lines of police
stand on the alert,
anticipating an attack on war
by women.

Women on the dead-end road
with drums and banners
dance for survival

in the face of violence.
Women disturb the orderly conduct
of the earth's destruction,
singing 'no more war!'

▮▮ NILENE O. A. FOXWORTH, USA

LIKE AN ORCHID IN DEEP MUDDY WATER
(From the shores of Bagamoyo)

when i first set foot
on black african soil
i walked with a soft gallant sway
as if tipping on gold coated diamonds
i felt like chasing butterflies
and bathing the hump of a camel
or singing 'i've got a home'
on the back of an elephant
as we dawdle across the continent

i wanted to toss seeds to crown pigeons
and dance barefooted on virgin soil
i wanted to hug little old wise men
and cornroll the hair of sweet old ladies
i wanted to sprout a miracle tongue
to spurt out 'asante mungu' in swahili
meaning 'thank you god'
i wanted to give my last dollar
to street beggars who cried, 'msaada'
meaning 'help'

i wanted to shout out loud
'freeeeee at last'
but in the midst of an obscure scene
i could visualize blood spots
trickling through the bush
trailing the footsteps
of courageous beloved ones

then my dreams died
and my weeping petals wilted
like an orchid
in deep muddy water

▟▟ LOURDES CASAL, born 1936, Cuba
(translated by Margaret Randall)

I LIVE IN CUBA

I live in Cuba.
I've always lived in Cuba
Even when I thought I existed
far from the painful crocodile
I've always lived in Cuba.
Not on the easy island
of violent
blues
and superb palms
but on the other,
the one that raised its head
on Hatuey's indomitable breath,
that grew
in passages and conspiracies,
that staggers and moves forward
in the building of socialism,
the Cuba whose heroic people lived through the sixties
and didn't falter,
who's been
darkly, silently
making history
and remaking herself.

// NOÉMIA DA SOUSA, born 1927, Mozambique
(translated from Portuguese by Margaret Dickenson)

IF YOU WANT TO KNOW ME

If you want to know me
examine with careful eyes
this bit of black wood
which some unknown Makonde brother
cut and carved
with his inspired hands
in the distant lands of the North.

This is what I am
empty sockets despairing of possessing life
a mouth torn open in an anguished wound
huge hands outspread
and raised in imprecation and in threat
a body tattooed with wounds seen and unseen
from the harsh whip strokes of slavery
tortured and magnificent
proud and mysterious
Africa from head to foot
this is what I am.

If you want to understand me
come, bend over this soul of Africa
in the black dockworker's groans
the Chopez' frenzied dances
the Changanas' rebellion
in the strange sadness which flows
from an African song, through the night.

And ask no more
to know me
for I'm nothing but a shell of flesh
where Africa's revolt congealed
its cry pregnant with hope.

Changanas — people of the Limpopo river basin.

IRINA RATUSHINSKAYA, born 1954, USSR
(translated by David McDuff)

THE WHITE-HOT BLIZZARD

The white-hot blizzard
Brands us with Russia.
Black rhetoric of craters,
Dark hollows under the snow:
Go away, eyeless woman, go away!
Only how are we to leave each other,
In our infinite whirling,
In our kinship and conflict with her?
And when at last you break loose
From the oppressive tenderness
Of her despotic embraces,
In which to fall asleep is to do so forever:
Your head swims,
As from the first childish drag at a cigarette,
And your lungs are torn to shreds
Like a cheap envelope.
And then, as you wait for everything that
Has emerged alive from her unpeopled cold
To recover from the narcosis –
To know that the angels of Russia
Freeze to death towards morning
Like sparrows in the frost
Falling from their wires into the snow.

▟▟ CH'IU CHIN, 1879?–1907, China
(translated by Kenneth Rexroth and Ling Chung)

TO THE TUNE 'THE RIVER IS RED'

How many wise men and heroes
Have survived the dust and dirt of the world?
How many beautiful women have been heroines?
There were the noble and famous women generals
Ch'in Liang-yü and Shen Yün-yin.
Though tears stained their dresses
Their hearts were full of blood.
The wild strokes of their swords
Whistled like dragons and sobbed with pain.

The perfume of freedom burns my mind
With grief for my country.
When will we ever be cleansed?
Comrades, I say to you,
Spare no effort, struggle unceasingly,
That at last peace may come to our people.
And jewelled dresses and deformed feet
Will be abandoned.
And one day, all under heaven
Will see beautiful free women,
Blooming like fields of flowers,
And bearing brilliant and noble human beings.

▟▟ ANOMA KANIÉ, Ivory Coast
(translated from French by Kathleen Weaver)

ALL THAT YOU HAVE GIVEN ME AFRICA

All that you have given me Africa
Lakes, forests, misted lagoons
All that you have given me,
Music, dances, all night stories around a fire

158

All that you have etched in my skin
Pigments of my ancestors
Indelible in my blood
All that you have given me Africa
Makes me walk
With a step that is like no other
Hip broken under the weight of time,
Feet large with journeys,
All that you have left to me
Even this lassitude bound to my heels,
I bear it with pride on my forehead
My health is no more to be lost
And I go forward
Praising my race which is no better
Or worse than any other.
All that you have given me Africa,
Savannahs gold in the noonday sun
Your beasts that men call wicked,
Your mines, inexplicable treasures
Obsession of a hostile world
Your suffering for lost paradises,
All that, I protect with an unforgiving hand
As far as the clear horizons
So that your heaven-given task
May be safe forever.

// NILENE O. A. FOXWORTH, USA

YES, I AM AN AFRICAN WOMAN

Yes, I am an African woman.
I am the Eve of Adam.
I am Queen Hatshepsut.
I am Nefertiti.
And the fallen Heroes
Plus ancient Pharaohs
Are watching over me.

Yes, I am an African woman,
And like the rainbow,
I have embraced the world,
And given it my PRIMARY
HUMAN colours.

Yes, I am an African woman,
And I like the rainbow,
I have embraced the world,
And given it my PRIMARY
HUMAN colours.

I am Queen Nzinga.
I am Queen Amina.
I am Harriet Tubman.
I am Mbuya Nehanda.
And Behold! I've been pushed!
Down! to the ground!
With only my bare hands
To use as a cup.
But I have fought many wars,
Plus untold battles,
AND I ALWAYS PULL MYSELF BACK UP.

Yes, I am an African woman . . .
Standing tall, as a cypress tree.
I am fearless!
For my Heroes and Pharaohs
Are watching over me.

▟▛ DENISE LEVERTOV, born 1923, USA

CREDO
from 'Mass for the Day of St Thomas Didymus'

I believe the earth
exists, and
in each minim mote

of its dust the holy
glow of thy candle.
Thou
unknown I know,
thou spirit,
giver,
lover of making, of the
wrought letter,
wrought flower,
iron, deed, dream.
Dust of the earth,
help thou my
unbelief. Drift,
gray become gold, in the beam of
vision. I believe and
interrupt my belief with
doubt. I doubt and
interrupt my doubt with belief. Be,
belovéd, threatened world.
                    Each minim
mote.
                    Not the poisonous
luminescence forced
out of its privacy,
the sacred lock of its cell
broken. No,
the ordinary glow
of common dust in ancient sunlight.
Be, that I may believe. Amen.

▟▎ DINAH LIVINGSTONE, UK

PRAISE

Praise, that's it!
Rilke, *Orpheus Sonnets*

I praise sky,
not god for it, in it,
just itself this morning vast
fast variable sunfilled bowl,
where puffs float,
feathered streamers proceed,
high azure satisfies
a wide expanse of heather.

I praise heather,
not god for it, in it,
but its own intense colour,
light-crowned amethyst
peerless this year,
here on sloping sides,
hardly hills, lazy
all the way to the far wood.

I praise trees,
each one its own –
not god for it, in it –
shape, form, soul, material,
alive with secret growth,
praise be for ever.
I come from the sun
to the cool of the forest beautiful.

Heather over there
extends to the sea,
steep cliff deep in bell and ling,
heathland to its last stand,
with fragrant bracken,
occasional gorse dazzle,
then smell of the sea, its sound.
Look down now and it fills the gaze.

And because here
the sea has so much weather,
may be but is not always
sweet speedwell,
also a luminous hazy silver,
outspoken indigo, alto violet,
sometimes storm black yellow,
in a climate moody but temperate,
I praise it for that.

Today it looks the colour of eyes
greenish greyish blue and mutable,
troubled when truth proves difficult
but whose smile is harebell
to cheat death of its sting.
I praise them too
and though I know no one is god
thankfully, I praise
you; and you; and you.

// JEAN LIPKIN, born 1926, South Africa

CREDO

Take for the sake of example
This ample branch of roses
That leans toward an invert sky.
With a girdle of words
Limit to it alone
Single and total
Its own particular truth.
No co-state of blossom near
Nor link of root nor kin.
To tear one petal off
Nor add one shadow in.
The captured static arrests
The sight, the tact, the scent —

To sound pure truth
Its only bent;
To bind occasion from event.
. . . Our experiment fails.
From the dramatic cut
An ailing truth bleeds out.
Lies shocked from its essences
And so dies.

We need
A kind of acceptance
Short of blind
That to our limits
There be sent
The mercy of astonishment.

DAISY YAMORA, Nicaragua
(translated by James Black, Bernardo Garcia-Pandavenes and Cliff Ross)

SONG OF HOPE

One day the fields will be forever green
and the earth will be black, sweet and moist.
Our children will grow tall on her
and the children of our children.

And they will be as free as the trees
and the birds of the wilderness.

Each morning they will awake in the joy of having life
and will know that the earth was reconquered for them.
One day . . .

To-day we plough the parched fields
but each furrow is soaked with blood.

IRINA RATUSHINSKAYA, born 1954, USSR
(translated by David McDuff)

TO MY UNKNOWN FRIEND

Above my half of the world
The comets spread their tails.
In my half of the century
Half the world looks me in the eye.
In my hemisphere the wind's blowing,
There are feasts of plague without end.
But a searchlight shines in our faces,
And effaces the touch of death.
And our madness retreats from us,
And our sadnesses pass through us,
And we stand in the midst of our fates,
Setting our shoulders against the plague.
We shall hold it back with our selves,
We shall stride through the nightmare.
It will not get further than us – don't be afraid
On the other side of the globe!

JENNY JOSEPH, born 1932, UK

WATCHING A CHILD WATCHING A WITCH
from 'Derivations'

Don't think it won't come to you:
Groping in bags on the pavement outside the shop
Tipping everything out to desperately find
The three-times-replaced purse, key, glove.

But think this also:
She may once have been, as now you are,
An image of youth, a sweet fresh hopeful
Stamped on some old haggish wandering gaze.

165

POLITICAL ACTIVIST LIVING ALONE

I'm middle-aged,
a child;
live in a toy shop,
pub;
shall never stop
enjoying my mobile,
glass animals,
shot of rum,
disco lamp.

Life is so dun
drear
dread –
to have fun
at all
you need the odd drink
and shimmering thing.

Picketing;
agitating;
working;
trudging
sunday by sunday
from marble arch
to whitehall,
embankment,
paddington

for the right to work,
free speech,
equality of race,
sex,
species,
sheer survival –
this vital cause
or that –

you need a bit of
glitter,
liquor,
colour,
warming

when you get back
to your empty flat . . .

▐▐ ASTRA, born USA

NOW OR NEVER

seven years ago
at forty five
i knew it was time
for a rock bottom change
time to kick over my traces
time to stand my life on its head
time to sow my autonomous oats
time to put my money where my mouth was

because i couldn't bear not to
                              any longer
which is not to say
it happened in one night
or even in one year
by magic and by spells
aided by rational and sympathetic talk
with my family
(quite the contrary)
that it was trauma free
that i didn't have
insomnia   backache   guilt   anxiety   frantic fears
savage rages   homicidal scenes   suicidal sobbings
that for a long time i didn't become
someone unrecognisable
to myself

but it was literally
                    change or die

because of being middle aged
not despite it
because of knowing in my gut
time was jogging onwards
and i deserved something
                    better
                            for myself
                                    now

or never

// MARGE PIERCY, USA

MORNING ATHLETES
For Gloria Nardin Watts

Most mornings we go running side by side
two women in mid-lives jogging, awkward
in our baggy improvisations, two
bundles of rejects from the thrift shop.
Men in their zippy outfits run in packs
on the road where we park, meet
like lovers on the wood's edge and walk
sedately around the corner out of sight
to our own hardened clay road, High Toss.

Slowly we shuffle, serious, panting
but talking as we trot, our old honorable
wounds in knee and back and ankle paining
us, short, fleshy, dark haired, Italian
and Jew, with our full breasts carefully
confined. We are rich earthy cooks
both of us and the flesh we are working
off was put on with grave pleasure. We
appreciate each other's cooking, each
other's art, photographer and poet, jogging
in the chill and wet and green, in the blaze

168

of young sun, talking over our work,
our plans, our men, our ideas, watching
each other like a pot that might boil dry
for that sign of too harsh fatigue.

It is not the running I love, thump
thump with my leaden feet that only
infrequently are winged and prancing,
but the light that glints off the cattails
as the wind furrows them, the rum cherries
reddening leaf and fruit, the way the pines
blacken the sunlight on their bristles,
the hawk flapping three times, then floating
low over beige grasses,
                         and your company
as we trot, two friendly dogs leaving
tracks in the sand. The geese call
on the river wandering lost in sedges
and we talk and pant, pant and talk
in the morning early and busy together.

✦✦ CHRISTINE DONALD, Canada

POOR OLD FAT WOMAN

Poor old fat woman, whither bound?
Home to my hearth, kind sir, she said.
Poor old fat woman, living alone!
I live with a woman who loves me, she said.
Poor old fat woman, lonely and tired!
We've plans for this evening, sir, she said.
No husband for you, poor old fat woman, eh!
I've never wanted one, sir, she said.
Poor old fat woman, what do you want?
Nothing that you can give, sir, she said,
   And you're wasting your time
   And you're wasting mine
So push off and do something useful instead.

▋▋ LI CH'ING-CHAO, 1084–1151, China
(translated by Kenneth Rexroth and Ling Chung)

TO THE TUNE 'ETERNAL HAPPINESS'

The setting sun is molten gold.
The evening clouds form a jade disc.
Where is he?
The willows are soft in the thick mist.
A sad flute plays 'Falling Plum Blossoms.'
How many Springs have I known?
This Feast of Lights should be joyful.
The weather is calm and lovely.
But who can tell if it
Will be followed by wind and rain?
A friend sends her perfumed carriage
And high bred horses to fetch me.
I thank my old poetry and wine companion.
I remember the happy days in the lost capital.
We took our ease in the women's quarters.
The Feast of Lights was elaborately celebrated –
Golden jewelry, brocaded girdles,
New sashes, we competed
To see who was most smartly dressed.
Now I am withering away,
Wind blown hair, frosty temples.
I am embarrassed to go out this evening.
I prefer to stay beyond the curtains,
And listen to talk and laughter
I can no longer share.

YOLANDA ULLOA, born 1948, Cuba

SHORT BIOGRAPHY OF A WASHERWOMAN

Emilia
strung the lines of white laundry
toward the horizon
and the suds grew
leaving no trace between her hands

Emilia's back
curved
like a flower
in the heat of the day.
She passed, unhurried, between the laundry
then faded away.

DENISE LEVERTOV, born 1923, USA

OLD PEOPLE DOZING

Their thoughts are night gulls
following the ferry, gliding
in and out of the window light
and through the reflected wall there, the door
that holds at its center
an arabesque of foam
always at vanishing point,
                              night gulls
that drift on airstream, reverse, swoop
out of sight, return, memory
moving again through the closed door,
white and effortless, hungry.

171

▟▟ MICHELE ROBERTS, born 1949, UK

AFTER MY GRANDMOTHER'S DEATH

each day is a full
spool, and death winds me in
her foot tap, taps
rocking the cradle

death is mrs moon, death is a spry spinster
I am a thread the moon spins with
and I come reeling in from my grief-stricken dance

the moon puts silver on grandmother's eyes
in her nostrils she puts the cold perfume of death
– moonspider spinning shrouds and swaddling bands

my mother's womb spun me a fine cocoon
spun me round and out, death tugged
my umbilical cord, she grinned
and tied me into her weaving

the moon who eats babies on winter nights
has her dark face, and rubbery hands
but grandmother rescued me
and held me close, she shone
steady for me, then I felt so blessed

then death strode out
trawling, trawling
and grandmother was mackerel to her silver net

the womb is the house of death
and each woman
spins in death's web; as I inch
back to the light
death pays out the bright thread

// ELENI FOURTOUNI, Greece
(translated by Eleni Fourtouni)

EURYNOME

I feared your wrath Eurynome
my grandmother
when your ancient gnarled fingers
would reach to my child's
thighs, pinching obedience into
my flesh — my flesh
spawned from your
rebellious flesh

the hearth's too narrow
for the likes of you
from first light to last light
you roam your valleys
and scale your mountains
commanding fields to yield good harvest
      vineyards to grow sweet fruit
      saplings to turn into olive trees
the ravines resounding with
your song, your anger
with the first cry of your babes
born next to your
plow

you take death as you take life
with huge leaps and bounds
grieving
over the graves of your
children
eating from the fiery fruit
of the dead
to burn away your pain

leading the dance-circle again
with the black banner
of your mourning
you feed the beggars at your door
the guests at your table
you oversee
your storerooms with rows of
clay jars filled with olive oil
goat skins packed with cheese
wine caskets fermenting new wine
your power
spilling over, into
the dark dough of our
daily bread

you fed me
the black broth you brewed
from your
blood
briny olives and thyme honey
grandmother
and when you sat by the
west window, taking in
the Last Light
you gave me your last command

'Give to no man
your Time of Life'

// NILENE O. A. FOXWORTH, USA

LOVE

Will you love me when I'm old
When my eyelids sink behind my skull
When my blood is running cold
And my conversation dull

When my gawky gums send a trembling voice
And my hands shake from a lack of choice
When I am as arid as the desert
And my firm breast sags
Like an old empty laundry bag

Will you love me when I'm old
When my flesh goes back to Mother Earth
And my naked bones are disarrayed
And my soul calmly floats beside the bay
Forgotten by the carnal beings of yesterday
Through the meridian of the seas
Through the depths of the unknown
From a bird to a bee
Will you love me when I'm gone?

// ANON., Canada
(English translation by Armand Schwerner)

SONG OF THE OLD WOMAN
(From the Netsilik People)

all these heads these ears these eyes
around me
how long will the ears hear me?
and those eyes how long
will they look at me?
when these ears won't hear me anymore
when these eyes turn aside from my eyes
I'll eat no more raw liver with fat
and those eyes won't see me anymore
and my hair, my hair will have disappeared.

▰▰ SUSAN WALLBANK, born 1943, UK

Poem untitled

For her Birthday
things to touch that shine
her hand reaching into the bag of presents
searching past the fur
for the hard edges
capable of permeating
the haze of disassociation
in which she lives now
dark and undefined.

This is years after the split occurred
the turning point
when her body moved one way
her mind the other
when separation sent her muscles bones
and skin
into the future
where unguarded it declined
decayed prematurely
but released the soul as cell by cell
the power of memory and thought
was eased away.

A mother still
she lifts the glittering object to her face
with all the thrill of childhood.

▐▐ ANON., India

A FOLK SONG

Old age has come, my head is shaking
Sitting on a stool my mind repents too late
I have no mother now, no brother and no family
No one will take me into their home
Sitting on a stool I think
Too late, I think again
Life has become sorrow
More than can be borne
O earth, break open and take me in.
In my parents' kingdom
I played and danced
But in my own kingdom there is sorrow
O earth, break open and take me in.

▐▐ STEF PIXNER, UK

NEAR DEATH

Near death
she halts

bent, brown, ninety
smelling rank.

She's peeled
the family photos

from the walls
leaving pale patches

bare of dust
like the rubbed out patches

of her memory.

'Is it Saturday today?
day or night, is it?'

At last she's happy
the bitterness of unlived passions

rubbed out too.

Cunningly young
she smiles, bends

fiddles a red rose through my button hole.
'My darling girl!'

Its sharp stalk
tickles my skin

between my breasts.

// ANON., Southern Sohone song
(reworking by Mary Austin)

SONG OF AN OLD WOMAN
ABANDONED BY HER TRIBE

Alas, that I should die,
That I should die now,
I who know so much!

It will miss me,
The twirling fire stick;
The fire coal between the hearth stones,
It will miss me.

The Medicine songs,
The songs of magic healing;
The medicine herbs by the water borders,
They will miss me;
The basket willow,
It will miss me;
All the wisdom of women,
It will miss me.

Alas, that I should die,
Who know so much.

// JUANA DE IBARBOUROU, 1897–1979, Uruguay
(translated from Spanish by Marti Moody)

LIFE-HOOK

If I die, don't take me to the cemetery.
My grave is opening
right at the surface of the earth, near the laughing
clatter of some birdhouse,
near a fountain and its gossip.

Right at the surface, love. Almost above ground
where the sun can heat my bones, and my eyes
can climb the stems of plants to watch
the sunset, its fierce red lamp.

Right at the surface. So the passage
will be short. I already see
my body fighting to get back above the soil,
to feel the wind again.

I know my hands may never calm down.
The ghosts around me will be dim, juiceless, but my
    hands
will scratch like moles.

Sprout seeds for me. I want them growing
in the yellow chalk of my bones.
I'll climb the roots like a grey staircase, and watch you
from the purple lilies.

▗▖ MAYA ANGELOU, born 1928, USA

ON AGEING

When you see me sitting quietly,
Like a sack left on the shelf,
Don't think I need your chattering,
I'm listening to myself.
Hold! Stop! Don't pity me!
Hold! Stop your sympathy!
Understanding if you got it,
Otherwise I'll do without it!

When my bones are stiff and aching
And my feet won't climb the stair,
I will only ask one favor:
Don't bring me no rocking chair.

When you see me walking, stumbling,
Don't study and get it wrong.
'Cause tired don't mean lazy
And every goodbye ain't gone.
I'm the same person I was back then,
A little less hair, a little less chin,
A lot less lungs and much less wind,
But ain't I lucky I can still breathe in.

▗▖ ELIZABETH JENNINGS, born 1926, UK

ONE FLESH

Lying apart now, each in a separate bed,
He with a book, keeping the light on late,
She like a girl dreaming of childhood,
All men elsewhere – it is as if they wait
Some new event: the book he holds unread,
Her eyes fixed on the shadows overhead.

Tossed up like flotsam from a former passion,
How cool they lie. They hardly ever touch,
Or if they do it is like a confession
Of having little feeling – or too much.
Chastity awaits them, a destination
For which their whole lives were a preparation.

Strangely apart, yet strangely close together,
Silence between them like a thread to hold
And not wind in. And time itself's a feather
Touching them gently. Do they know they're old,
These two who are my father and my mother
Whose fire from which I came has now grown cold?

// GWENDOLYN BROOKS, born 1917, US

THE BEAN EATERS

They eat beans mostly, this old yellow pair.
Dinner is a casual affair.
Plain chipware on a plain and creaking wood,
Tin flatware.

Two who are Mostly Good.
Two who have lived their day,
But keep on putting on their clothes
And putting things away.

And remembering . . .
Remembering, with twinklings and twinges,
As they lean over the beans in their rented back room that
    is full of beads and receipts and dolls and clothes,
    tobacco crumbs, vases and fringes.

▟▟ SAPPHO, sixth century BC, Greece
(translated by Josephine Balmer)

Poem untitled

. . . already old age is wrinkling my
skin and my hair is turning from black
to grey; my knees begin to tremble
and my legs no longer carry me . . .
oh but once, once we were like young deer
. . . what can I do? . . .

                 . . . it is not possible
to return to my youth; for even
Eös, the dawn – whose arms are roses,
who brings light to the ends of the earth –
found that old age embraced Tithonus,
her immortal lover . . .
              . . . I know I must die . . .
yet I love the tenderness of life
and this and desire keep me here in
the brightness and beauty of the sun
[and not with Hades . . .]

*The text of the poem is very fragmentary and much of this translation is
conjectural. Eös, Tithonus: Eös, the dawn goddess, fell in love with Tithonus,
a mortal. She asked Zeus to give him immortality but forgot to ask for eternal
youth. Eventually he became old and shrivelled and talked endlessly. Eös
looked after him and finally turned him into the cicada. (Josephine Balmer)*

BIOGRAPHIES

Bella Akhmadulina was born in Moscow in 1937, of mixed Tartar–Italian descent. She has been married to three writers: Yevgeny Yevtushenko for a brief time, Yuri Nagibin, and finally Gennadi Mamlin. At one time she was unpopular with the authorities and expelled from the Gorky Institute of Literature because of her apolitical stance. However, she now enjoys great success as a writer both in Russia and abroad.

Anna Akhmatova (1889–1966) was born in Odessa, Russia, in 1889 and grew up in St Petersburg (now Leningrad). In 1910 she married Nicolai Gumiliev, the poet. Together they founded the Acmeist movement, which favoured classicism rather than symbolism. In 1921, three years after their divorce, Gumiliev was shot as a counter-revolutionary. At the beginning of the Stalinist purges, their son, Lev, was arrested and later sent to the labour camps and Anna Akhmatova found herself out of favour, denounced and expelled from the Writers' Union. After Stalin's death, her son was finally freed and she herself slowly 'rehabilitated'. She received an honorary degree from Oxford University in 1965 and died a year later.

Dazzly Anderson was born in Jamaica and emigrated to England in 1964. She started English classes at St Paul's centre and, encouraged by her tutor and her four children, joined the Women's Writing Group at the Albany Centre. Her greatest wish is to have her work published.

Maya Angelou, actress, author, civil-rights activist, composer, editor, film maker, lecturer, playwright, poet, producer, singer and teacher, was born Marguerite Johnson in St Louis, Missouri, in 1928. She has written about her life of achievement and intense activity in her five-volume autobiography published by Virago, which opens with *I Know Why the Caged Bird Sings*. She says that writing about herself is a painful process of 'dragging my pencil across the old scars to sharpen it'. She has also produced several volumes of poetry: *Just Give Me a Cool Drink of Water 'for I Diiie* (1971), *Oh Pray My Wings Are Gonna Fit Me Well* (1975), *And Still I Rise* (1978), *Shaker Why Don't You Sing?* (1983). A selection of the poems from the last two collections was published in 1986 by Virago under the title *And Still I Rise*. Maya Angelou has also collaborated with Tom Feelings on *Now Sheba Sings the Song* (Virago, 1987). In the 1960s she became involved in the black struggles, working closely with Martin Luther King. She now has a life-time appointment as Reynolds Professor of American Studies at Wake Forest University in North Carolina and lectures extensively all over America and abroad. 'I speak to the black experience . . . but I am always talking about the human condition – about what we can endure, dream, fail at and still survive.'

Margaret Atwood was born in Ontario in 1939. She has lectured at many universities and has also been Writer-in-Residence at the universities of Toronto and Tuscaloosa, Alabama. In addition she has worked as a cashier, a summer-camp counsellor, waitress and film-script writer. Margaret Atwood is Canada's most eminent novelist, poet and critic. She has won numerous awards for her work which has been translated into fifteen languages. Her first novel *The Edible Woman* was published in 1969, followed by *Surfacing* in 1972, *Lady Oracle* in 1976, *Life Before Man* in 1979 and *Bodily Harm* in 1982; all these novels are published in paperback by Virago. Her most recent novel, *The Handmaid's Tale* (1985), was shortlisted for the Booker Prize, won the Governor-General's Award in 1986 and the Arthur C. Clarke prize for science fiction in 1987. A poet of world-wide reputation, her first volume, *The Circle Game* (1966), won the Governor-General's Award. Since then she has published many volumes of poetry – *The Animals in That Country* (1968), *The Journals of Susanna Moodie* (1970), *Procedures for Underground* (1970), *Oratorio for Sasquatch, Man and Two Androids, Poems for Voices* (1970), *Power Politics* (1971), *You Are Happy* (1974), *Marsh Hawk* (1977), *Two-Headed Poems* (1978), *True Stories* (1981), *Notes Towards a Poem That Can Never Be Written* (1981), *Interlunar* (1984) and *Selected Poems II* (1986). Margaret Atwood has a young daughter and lives in Toronto.

Pat Arrowsmith has worked as assistant editor at Amnesty International for fifteen years. She has also worked full time in the peace movement, having been actively involved in the nuclear-disarmament movement since 1957. She has been a political prisoner eleven times. She draws and paints and has often exhibited her work. Published works include *Jericho, Somewhere Like This, The Prisoner* (fiction); *To Asia in Peace, The Colour of Six Schools* (non-fiction); *Breakout, On the Brink, Thin Ice* (poems and pictures). 'Political Activist' first appeared in *Peace News* in 1984.

Astra was born in New York in 1927 and grew up during the Depression on the East Coast. She says that the watersheds in her life have been motherhood and feminism, which occurred at more or less the same time. For the last twenty-five years she has lived in England where she at first suffered greatly from isolation. However, on joining a women's group her life style and politics were irrevocably altered and she took up writing seriously as a poet. In her work she writes both for and about women's liberation. Some poems are about herself; mostly they are concerned with women she has admired and encouraged and those for whom she has grieved and from whom she has gained strength. Her poetry has appeared in many anthologies, among them *One Foot on the Mountain, Hard Feelings* and *Bread and Roses* (Virago). She has also published three collections of her own work, *Fighting Words, Battle Cries* and *Back You Come, Mother Dear* (Virago).

Himani Bannerji was born in what was then East Pakistan. She was educated and later taught in Calcutta. In 1969 she went to Canada, where she now lives. She teaches Social Science at York University in Toronto and has had poems published in *Canadian Women Poets* (a feminist quarterly). Her most recent publication is a book of poems, *Doing Time*.

Maria Banus was born in 1914. She grew up in Bucharest and studied at the Faculty of Letters and Law. As well as writing poetry – ten publications – and four plays, she has published her translations of the works of many poets. She has received the Romanian State Prize Laureate.

Valerie Bloom was born in Jamaica, where she grew up and trained as a teacher. After college she taught and started a speech and drama club. In England she has taught and lectured on the folk traditions in poetry, dance and song and has also worked on radio. She now attends Kent University. Her book of poetry, *Touch Mi; Tell Mi!*, was published 1983.

Gwendolyn Brooks was born in 1917 in Kansas but grew up in Chicago. She is a major writer and has published, since 1945, nine books of poetry, a novel and part of an autobiography. In 1949 she was awarded the Pulitzer Prize for *Annie Allen*. She has also gained two Guggenheim fellowships, the American Arts and Letters Award and, in 1968, was named poet laureate of Illinois.

Jennifer Brown is a radio producer and a journalist. Her poems have been published in *Caribbean Quarterly, Arts Review, Jamaica Journal,* the *Jamaica Daily News, Africa Woman,* and in an anthology, *The Caribbean Poem.*

Dinah Butler was born in 1960 to an English mother and absent Nigerian father. She grew up in London, then taught in Kenya for two years before studying social anthropology at Sussex University. She now does community work with pensioners, takes creative writing workshops, is training as a therapist and, in 1987, is expecting a baby.

Lourdes Casal (1936–1981) was born in Havana. When the revolution broke out, she left for the United States where 'I didn't fit in anywhere . . . because I'm black, a woman and Latin'. She participated in the struggle against racial discrimination and the war in Vietnam. She had been opposed to the revolution originally, and in America she linked herself with other exiled Cubans, many of whom were troubled by their vision of the revolution. Lourdes was one of the first to contact the Cuban authorities and gain permission to travel to Cuba where she researched and wrote about her country. In 1974/5 she won a Cintas Foundation Grant in literature. She has published several books on the literature of, and the revolution in, Cuba, as well as her own poetry and short stories.

Nina Cassian was born in Galati, Romania, in 1924. She is a prolific writer and since 1946 has published fifty volumes of poetry, translations, children's verse, and short stories. She is also a composer. In 1982, three of her chamber works were performed in New York. Her most recent publication is a collection of poems, *Countdown,* and her most recent enterprise is a children's play, which she wrote and set to music.

Nurunnessa Choudhury was born in Sylhet, Bangladesh, in 1943. She was brought up in a liberal family atmosphere and soon became involved in the movement for national emancipation. She was the first woman to be arrested and put on trial for her political activities. After Bangladesh achieved independence, she founded and ran a home for women and children displaced by the civil war. Later, disillusioned with the new regime, she became active in the new opposition group. Her criticisms were outspoken and she was deprived of her citizenship. She now lives in London with her husband and three children. She has published poetry in Bengali weeklies and magazines, a selection of poems in *Nakhatrer Protikhai* (Anticipating a Star), a novel, *Gangchill* (Seagull), and a collection of poems in a dual-text publication, *I See Cleopatra and Other Poems.*

Ch'iu Chin (1879–1907) was married at eighteen. After the births of her children, she left her family in 1904 to study in Tokyo. There she joined Sun Yat-Sen's revolutionary party, and the following year returned to China. In 1906 she founded a newspaper for women in Shanghai. She then took a post as teacher at a school which served as a secret headquarters for the revolutionary party. She was arrested and tried by the Manchu government. At her trial, her poems were used in evidence against her. She was found guilty of treason and beheaded.

Cheryl Clarke was born in Washington, DC, in 1947. Since 1979, her book reviews, essays, poems and short stories have appeared in numerous small press publications: *Sinister Wisdom, Conditions, Ikon,* the *American Voice,* the *New York Narrative, Black Scholar, Thirteenth Moon, Hanging Loose.* Her poems have been published in several anthologies: *Home Girls: A Black Feminist Anthology, This Bridge Called Me Back, Lesbian Poetry.* Her first publication of her own collection of poems is *Narratives: Poems in the Tradition* and her most recent publication is *Living as a*

Lesbian. She is part of a collective editorial body of *Conditions*, a magazine of writing by women with an emphasis on lesbian writers. She considers her lesbianism the filter of her imagination.

Michelle T. Clinton is part of the political artists' community of Los Angeles. Her proud and angry feminist performance art has addressed the issues of child abuse, rape and South African apartheid. Her first volume of poetry was *High Blood/Pressure*, 1986. Scheduled for release in 1987 is *Black/Angeles*, which consists of her poetry and that of Wanda Coleman, the award-winning poet.

Jayne Cortez was born in Arizona, grew up in California and is currently living in New York City. Her poetry has been published in many journals, magazines, and anthologies including *Confirmation, Powers of Desire, New Black Voices, Giant Talk, Free Spirits, Presence Africaine, Mundus Artium* and the Unesco *Courier*. She is the author of six books of poetry and four recordings. Her most recent collection is *Coagulations: New and Selected Poems* and her most recent recording, *Maintain Control*. She has lectured and read her poetry alone and with music throughout the United States, West Africa, Europe, Latin America and the Caribbean.

Christine Craig studied at the University of the West Indies. She has had poems and stories published in the *Savacou* and *Arts Review*. She has also written for radio and television, including a film script, *Women in Crises*. Her publications include two children's books, *Emmanuel Goes to Market* and *Emmanuel and His Parrot*. Some of her poetry appears in *Jamaica Woman: An Anthology of Poems*. 'I write, I am a feminist, I am a mother. I am a Jamaican woman. That's all the important things.'

Charmaine Crowell, born in Virginia, is an experienced performer, director, playwright, poet and storyteller. She is a member of the Black Actors' Workshop at the American Conservatory Theatre in San Francisco and the African American Drama Company of California. She directed the Black Theatre Workshop at San José City College and also works with children's theatre as actor, teacher and director. Her first collection of poems was published recently under the title *Tell Them to Call You Cactus Flower*. She is married and has two children.

Christine Donald says of herself, 'I'm thirty years English and six years Canadian and just beginning to see life as my own. For a long time, I thought words were the most trustworthy things in the world and I was backed in this by receiving a "sound classical education". Then there was women. And feminism. Words have grown a lot richer for this – and so have I.' Her publications include *The Fat Woman Measures Up* (1986) and *The Breaking Up Poems* (1987).

Mary Dorcey was born in County Dublin, Eire. She has travelled widely and lived in England, France, America and Japan, and worked in a variety of jobs including disc jockey, waitress, restaurateur and English-language teacher. She has been active in the women's movement since 1972 and was a founder member of Irishwomen United. Her first book of poetry, *Kindling*, was published in 1982. Since then her work has appeared in many journals and been anthologised in *Bread and Roses* (Virago), *In the Pink, Beautiful Barbarians, Contemporary Poets*. She now lives in Ireland, dividing her time between County Kerry and Dublin. She is a working on a novel and a collection of short stories.

U. A. Fanthorpe now lives in Gloucestershire. Of her writing she says, 'I always meant to be a writer . . . I've been in love with the English language since I first learned to speak, and I enjoy finding out answers. My poems are mostly, in one way or another, an attempt to deal with an area of darkness in my mind. I'm not able to shed light on the darkness, but it seems important to try. When the poems don't work, it is generally because of a bad habit of putting cheap wit before love.' Her first job was as a teacher, then she decided to escape the profession for which she 'had no temperament' and became a clerk/receptionist at a small hospital. 'Poetry struck during my first month behind the desk. I think it started because of the rage and frustration I felt.' Her publications include *Side Effects* (1978), *Standing To* (1982), *Voices Off* (1984), *Selected Poems* (1986). *A Watching Brief* will be published in 1987.

Elaine Feinstein was born in Lancashire in 1930. She went to Cambridge University and lives there now. Her publications include *In a Green Eye* (1966), *The Magic Apple Tree* (1971), *The Celebrants* (1973), *Some Unease and Angels* (1977) and *The Feast of Eurydice* (poetry); *Children of the Rose* (1975), *The Ecstasy of Dr Miriam Garner* (1976), *The Survivors* (1982) and *The Border* (1984) (fiction). She is noted for translations of the Russian poet, Marina Tsvetayeva.

Teresita Fernández was born in Santa Clara, Cuba, in 1930 and educated at Catholic schools. Deeply influenced by her mother's musical ability, she sang as soon as she could speak and started to write poetry at the age of thirteen (a legacy from her father). She trained as a teacher. When the revolution broke out, she joined the rebels and afterwards went to Havana where she launched two children's shows on television and played and sang in restaurants and bars. In the sixties she worked for the Ministry of Culture. Later she travelled through the country, performing for the mine-workers, cane-cutters and others. With Francisco Garzon Gespedes, she revived the troubadour tradition, meeting each Sunday in a park to sing, recite and tell stories. She has recorded some of her settings of verse to music. And for International Children's Year, her setting of Gabriela Mistral's 'Give Me Your Hand and We'll Dance' was sung by 4500 children.

Eleni Fourtouni was born in Sparta, Greece. In 1953 she went to America as an exchange student. After graduation, she married and for the next fifteen years was immersed in bringing up her daughter and son. For 1987 she is in Greece researching Greek women and justice – 'injustice, I should say'. Her publications include *Greek Women Poets, Four Greek Women/Love Poems* (translations), *Monovassia, Watch the Flame* (original poetry), and *Greek Women in Resistance Journals – Oral Histories* (translated, selected and introduced).

Nilene O. A. Foxworth. Poet, author and political activist, Nilene Foxworth is one of Black America's most eloquent recitalists. Her poetic style seeks to 'make the heart strong and the soul smile'. During the 1977 Black and African World Festival, in which she participated, she was presented with her 'new names' (Omodele and Adeoti). In 1979, she was asked to become a member of the Union of Writers of the African Peoples. She has written, produced and directed a television show, 'The Indigenous Woman'. Her publications include *Bury Me in Africa* and *Whose Independence and Whose Liberty*. 'Most of my adult life has been a commitment to my people, but I owe it to myself to learn about my African heritage, which was denied Blacks for centuries . . . I have made my sojourn to the homeland (Africa) every two years for the past twelve years . . . It is my dream to see my people free and independent to govern themselves and their innate boundaries; and they will be free, because exploiters can destroy the "physical" world, but they can never destroy the "spiritual" elements led By God.'

Kath Fraser was born in London in 1947. She is a 'lesbian, able-bodied non-mother, with christian origins. Many past identities, the present one is nearly forty. I live in east Lancashire, intending to move along the road into west Yorkshire. Locating myself in time and place seems to be of first importance right now.'

187

Katherine Gallagher was born in Maldon, Victoria, Australia, in 1935. She started writing poetry in 1965 and now lives in London. 'Poetry is a way of seeing, of making order out of turbulences. I can't imagine my life without poetry and trying to write it . . .' Her publications include *The Eye's Circle* (1975), *Tributaries of the Lovesong* (1978) and *Passengers to the City* (1985).

Nikki Giovanni, poet, recording artist, lecturer, has been called the Princess of Black Poetry. She has received numerous awards and honorary doctorates from several universities. Her publications of poetry include *Black Feeling Black Talk* (1968), *Black Judgement* (1969), *Re:Creation* (1970), *Night Comes Softly* (1970), *Spin a Soft Black Song* (children's poetry, 1971), *My House* (1972), *Ego Tripping and Other Poems for Young Readers* (1973), *The Women and the Men* (1975), *Cotton Candy on a Rainy Day* (1978), *Vacation Time* (1979), *Those Who Ride the Night Wind*. She has also published *A Dialogue: James Baldwin and Nikki Giovanni* (1972), *A Poetic Equation: Conversations between Nikki Giovanni and Margaret Walker* (1974), *Gemini* (essays, 1971).

Carole E. Gregory is now teaching writing at the Borough of Manhattan Community College and at New York University. She has recently finished a poetry book entitled *For a Lifetime*, to be published.

Gillian E. Hanscombe was born in Melbourne, Australia, in 1945 and has lived in England since 1969. She has written and co-authored half a dozen books. For the last three years she has worked in the freelance partnership of Cameron and Hanscombe, producing educational and commercial written materials. She has an eleven-year-old son and wants 'above all to stay at home with my lover and write verse'. Publications include *Hecate's Charms* (1976), and *Flesh and Paper* (poems written with Suniti Namjoshi). Her poems have appeared in many anthologies, including *Bread and Roses* (Virago, 1982), and *Beautiful Barbarians* (1986).

Frances E. W. Harper (1825–1911) was born in Maryland. Her parents died when she was three and she was brought up by an uncle and educated at the school he ran for free black people. She became deeply involved in the issue of slavery and in 1854 she began a series of lectures against its evils. After the Civil War, she continued to lecture, this time insisting on the need for education among the newly freed slaves. Her publications included *Atlanta Offering Poems* (1895), *Eventide* (1854), *Forest Leaves*, *Idylls of the Bible*, *Iola Leroy: Or Shadows Uplifted* (1892), *Moses: A Story of the Nile* (1889). She also published many poems and articles in *The Liberator*.

Maureen Hawkins lives in England and is a founder member of the Munirah Theatre Company. She has been involved in community theatre for several years. Most recently her poems have appeared in the anthology *Watchers and Seekers* (1987).

Huang Ho (1498–1569) was the daughter of the President of the Board of Works of the Ming Court. She married Yang Shen, a poet/dramatist. She was unusual in that she wrote erotic verse – this was normally the province of courtesans.

Juana de Ibarbourou was born in Uruguay in 1895. At the age of 18 she married an army officer and they had one son. Her first collection of poetry, *Las Lenguas de diamante* (Diamond Tongues), caused a great sensation. By 1929 her prestige as a poet had grown so great that she was given the name of 'Juana de America'.

Lady Ise (c. 875–938) served as a lady-in-waiting to Emperor Uda's consort Onshi. She was a celebrity and, being one of the Emperor's favourites, bore him a son. Later she had a liaison with one of his other sons and gave birth to a daughter.

Elizabeth Jennings was born in 1926 in Lincolnshire and went to school and university in Oxford. She has travelled extensively all over England, and to Florence, Edinburgh and New York, to read her poetry. Her interests include the theatre, travelling in Italy and collecting. She has written sixteen books of poetry, including *A Way of Looking,* (1955), *A Sense of the World* (1958), *Song for a Birth or a Death* (1961), *Recoveries* (1964), *The Mind Has Mountains* (1966), *Growing Points* (1975), *Consequently I Rejoice* (1977), *Moments of Grace* (1979), *Celebration and Elegies* (1982), *Collected Poems 1953–1986.* She has also translated Michelangelo's sonnets and written two books of children's verse and five prose works.

Jenny Joseph was born in 1932 and read English at Oxford. Her publications of poetry include *The Unlooked-for Season* (1960), for which she won the Gregory Award, *Rose in the Afternoon* (1974) which won the Cholmondeley Award, *The Thinking Heart* (1978), *Beyond Descartes* (1983), and *Persephone* (1986), a fiction in prose and verse. For this last work she was awarded the 1986 James Tait Black Prize for fiction.

Judith Kazantzis was born in 1940. She wrote poetry as a child and started again after 'marriage, children, painting, psychoanalysis, the Labour Party and the Women's Movement'. Her publications include *The Wicked Queen* (1980), *Touch Papers* with Michèle Roberts and Michelene Wandor (1982), *Let's Pretend* (Virago, 1984), *A Poem for Guatemala* (1986). 'I also paint, and spend time in the US. Issues of equality are what concern me, also what I see.'

Anna Maria Lenngren (1754–1819) was born in Sweden, the daughter of a university professor. She received a classical education and was well known for her translations of Latin poetry and drama. Gifted with musical talent and a beautiful voice, she composed many songs. Her poems were published in the *Stockholms Posten*, which was edited by her husband. At her express wish, her poems were not collected until after her death when they were published under the title *A Poetry Attempt.*

Denise Levertov was born in Ilford, Essex, in 1923. She served as a nurse in the Second World War. Soon after this, she married the writer Mitchell Goodman and they had one son. She emigrated to the United States and was naturalised in 1955. She has lectured at many universities and received numerous awards, honorary doctorates and fellowships. Her publications of poetry include *The Double Image* (1946), *Here and Now* (1957), *Overland to the Islands* (1958), *With Eyes at the Back of Our Heads* (1959), *O Taste and See* (1964), *The Jacob's Ladder* (1965), *The Sorrow Dance* (1968), *Penguin Modern Poets*, with Kenneth Rexroth and William Carlos Williams (1967), *Relearning the Alphabet* (1970), *To Stay Alive* (1971), *Footprints* (1972), *The Freeing of the Dust* (1975), *Life in the Forest* (1978), *Candles in Babylon* (1982), *Oblique Prayers* (1984), *Breathing the Water* (1987).

Deborah Levy is a playwright, poet and writer of short stories. Her work for the theatre includes *Pax* for the Women's Theatre Group, *Clam* for Blood Group and *Heresies* for the Royal Shakespeare Company. She was born in 1959 and lives in London.

Lady Anne Lindsay (1750–1825) was the author of the popular ballad 'Auld Robin Gray' (1771). Later during her residence in South Africa she wrote, under her married name, the journals *Lady Anne Barnard at the Cape, 1797–1802.*

Jean Lipkin was born in Johannesburg in 1926. She was educated in Pretoria and at Witwatersrand University. In 1960 she left Johannesburg with her husband and two children and now lives in London. Of her poetry she says, 'A real poem is something more than the sum of its technical parts. This is the unbidden, unbiddable thing (grace, mystery, inspiration?) that goes beyond the limitations of the poet and the language. I can only hope this will sometimes be granted to me.' Her poems have been published in *Africa South* and *Contrast* and have been read on BBC Radio. *Among Stones* (1975) was her first book of poems. In 1986 she published a new collection, *With Fences Down*.

Dinah Livingstone grew up in England's West Country. She now lives in London, has three children and is a poetry tutor and translator in adult education. She has recited her poems in London and elsewhere. Her work has been broadcast and published in magazines, anthologies and pamphlets by Katabasis, and has won Arts Council awards in 1969, 1975 and 1978. The latest of these are *Love in Time* (1982), *Glad Rags* (1983), *Something Understood* (1985), *Soul in Paraphrase*, a set of seven poems with woodcuts by J. Kingsley Cook (1987), and *Saving Grace, new and selected poems 1967–87* (1987). Her poems have 'to do with struggling to be free of dictators, for a feminism which can be seen as erotic, maternal and/or eccentric as it likes, and a socialism where the political fully respects the personal, women and men in their intractable particularity'.

Audre Lorde was born in 1934 and lives in New York. Her publications include *The First Cities, Cables to Rage, From a Land Where Other People Live, The New York Head Shop and Museum, Coal, Between Ourselves, The Black Unicorn, The Cancer Journals. Zami – A New Spelling of my Name, Chosen Poems – Old and New, Sister Outsider* and, most recently, *Our Dead Behind Us*.

Mary Mackey was born in Indianapolis in the United States and is related through her family to Mark Twain. She went to Harvard and later received a Ph.D. in comparative literature from the University of Michigan. At present she is a professor of English and writer in residence at California State University, Sacramento. Publications include *Split Ends, One Night Stand, Skin Deep, The Dear Dance of Eros* (poetry); *McCarthy's List, The Last Warrior Queen, The Grand Passion, The Kindness of Strangers* (novels).

Desanka Maksimovic was born in 1898 in Rabrovica near Valjevo. She studied in Belgrade and Paris, then returned to Belgrade where she taught for many years and wrote poetry. Her post-war books of poetry include (translated titles), *Poet and His Native Land, The Scent of the Earth, I Seek Mercy* and *I Have No More Time*.

Zindziswa Mandela was born in South Africa in 1959, the younger daughter of Winnie and Nelson Mandela. A collection of her poems, *Black as I Am*, was published in California in 1978.

Sandy McIntosh has worked as a reporter for the *Jamaican Daily News* and won several awards for her journalism. Her short stories and poems have been published in the *Gleaner, Children's Own* and *Swing*.

Gabriela Mistral (1889–1957) was born in Vicuña, Chile. 'Gabriela Mistral' was a pseudonym, Lucila Godoy Alcayaga her real name. She first received recognition for her literary gifts while still a schoolteacher with her publication of *Sonetos de Muerte*. She was honoured as a poet throughout her life and in 1945 was awarded the Nobel Prize for Literature.

Nancy Morejón was born in 1944 in Havana where she still lives. She studied language and French literature at the University of Havana. Her publications include *Silences* (1962), *Love, Attributed City* (1964), *Richard Brought his Flute* (1967), *Parameters of an Epoch* (1979), *Essential October* (1983), *Grenada Notebook* (1984), *Poems* (selected) (1980), *In Praise of Dance* (1982), *Where the Island Sleeps Like a Wing*, translated by Kathleen Weaver (1985). Her poetry has been translated into various languages and appeared in many anthologies.

Mwana Kupona Msham was born in East Africa early in the nineteenth century and died in 1860. Her most famous poem was 'Poem to her Daughter'. In spite of its length, the poem (and the poet) was held in such esteem that many learned it by heart.

Mririda n'Ait Attik was born in Morocco. During the 1940s she was a courtesan and famous for the strange, beautiful songs that she sang. These were based on the traditional life of the valley and composed in the Berber dialect.

Suniti Namjoshi was born in Bombay, India, in 1941. She has published *The Jackass and the Lady* (1980), *Feminist Fables* (1981), *From the Bedside Book of Nightmares* (1984), *The Conversations of Cow* (1985), *Aditi and the One-Eyed Monkey* (1986), and *Flesh and Paper*, written with Gillian Hanscombe (1986).

Rafaela Chacón Nardi was born in Cuba in 1926. She has written poetry all her life and published three books. She has worked as a teacher, for UNESCO and has represented the Cuban revolutionary government at UNESCO events. Recently she has been actively involved in the field of education and was awarded the Orden Nacional and the Frank Pais Medal for this work.

Taiwo Olaleye-Oruene was born in Lagos, Nigeria. She has lived in England since attending secondary school and university here. She is a lawyer and has several publications to her credit.

Grace Nichols was born in 1950 in Guyana where she grew up. She came to Britain in 1977 and since then has published several children's books, including *Leslyn in London*, as well as two collections of poetry. Her first, *i is a long memoried woman*, was the winner of the 1983 Commonwealth Poetry Prize, and her second, *The Fat Black Woman's Poems*, was published by Virago in 1984. Her poems have also appeared in *Frontline*, *Ambit*, *Kunapipi*, *Poetry Review* and, most recently, the anthology *Watchers and Seekers*. She published her first adult novel, *Whole of a Morning Sky* (Virago), in 1986.

Otomo no Sakanoe no Iratsume was born in Japan in the eighth century into a literary family. Many of her relations were poets, including her nephew, the famous Otomo no Yakamochi, whom her daughter, also a poet, married.

Rita Boumi-Pappas was born in Greece. A prolific and passionately concerned poet, she published her first collection of poems in 1930 followed by a further sixteen publications in later years. In *A Thousand Murdered Girls* she focused on the young women in the Greek resistance during the Second World War who were executed when they refused to sign 'declarations of repentance and good behaviour'. In her introduction she wrote, 'These executed girls are my daughters, your daughters, daughters of all real people . . . they did not die to be silent'.

Marge Piercy was born in Detroit, Michigan. She travels widely, giving readings of her poetry. She has actively supported anti-war and civil rights groups and been closely involved with the women's movement. Publications include *Going Down Fast, Dance the Eagle to Sleep, Small Changes, Woman on the Edge of Time* (fiction); *Breaking Camp, Hard Loving, To Be of Use, The Twelve-Spoked Wheel Flashing, The Moon is Always Female, Living in the Open* (poetry).

Christine de Pisan (c. 1364–1430) was born in France and married at the age of fifteen to Etienne de Castel. Although the marriage was arranged by her father, it was deeply happy and she wrote intimately about it in a way that was rare at that time. Both her father and husband worked for the court of Charles V but on the king's death in 1380 her father was reduced to poverty, and, soon after, her husband died. Suddenly she was alone with three children to support, which she did by means of her writing. She was an early defender of the rights of women and wrote a treatise on their education. She finally retired to a convent, where she wrote a work in praise of Joan of Arc.

Stef Pixner was born in 1945 and brought up in London. Apart from writing and publishing poetry, she has worked as a polytechnic lecturer, waitress, artist's model, gardener and feminist therapist. Her work has appeared in several anthologies: *Hard Feelings* (1979), *Licking the Bed Clean* (1978), *Smile Smile Smile Smile* (1980) and *Bread and Roses* (Virago, 1982). In 1985 Virago published a collection of her poetry, *Sawdust and White Spirit*.

Wendy Poussard was born in Melbourne, Australia, in 1943. She is married and has four children. After a nomadic beginning, the family now live in East St Kilda. Wendy Poussard is executive officer of International Women's Development Agency, a community-based organisation which works with women's groups in other countries on projects ranging from policy research to digging lavatories. Besides poetry she has written many books, articles and songs, and has also written for television and radio. She says that her writing has been influenced by Asian people and politics and the international women's movement. Her first collection of poetry was *Outbreak of Peace: Poems and Notes from Pine Gap* (1984).

Marsha Prescod came to England as a small child in the 1950s from the Caribbean. She lives and works in London.

Margaret Randall is a writer, poet, photographer, teacher, oral historian, feminist and author of forty books. In 1986, Margaret Randall was denied permanent resident status during a hearing before the US Immigration and Naturalization Service. It was claimed that her writings advocated communism and two books were particularly used to support this – *Part of a Solution/Portrait of a Revolution*, in which she spoke positively about women's rights in present-day Cuba, and *The Spirit of the People*, a book of interviews with Vietnamese women. Margaret Randall, a true poet, simply writes what she sees and what she hears: 'I tried to understand the Cuban revolutionary process but always as an outsider, a foreigner . . . today I would probably say I was a humanist before I would say I was a Marxist, although I certainly use Marxism as a tool, at least to understand.' She was born in New York in 1936, but grew up in Albuquerque. In 1961, back in New York, tired of living as a single parent and trying to write and earn a living, she moved to Mexico City. Here she married the poet Sergio Mondrago and later became a Mexican citizen in order to obtain employment. She and her husband began the bilingual literary magazine *El Corno Emplumado*. In the 1960s the magazine took a strong line against the Mexican government's repression of the student movement. Margaret Randall was harassed; troops stormed her house and took her passport, and she went into hiding. Fearing for their safety, she sent her children to Cuba and later followed them. She lived there for ten years and, from interviews with many women, wrote *Women in Cuba* and *Cuban Women Now*. After twenty-three years in Latin America, she returned to Albuquerque, where her ageing parents live, and applied for permanent residency. Her struggle continues. Other publications include *Inside the Nicaraguan Revolution*, *Carlota: Prose and Poems from Havana* and *Breaking the Silences*, her translations of twentieth-century poetry by Cuban women.

Irina Ratushinskaya was born in 1954, in Odessa, USSR. She has recently been released from a 'strict regime' labour camp for 'especially dangerous state criminals' where she had been for four years. She was imprisoned for persistently resisting social injustice and for writing about what she saw with a blazing truth. She began to believe in God at an early age and was often involved in conflicts at school. In spite of this, she went to university, where she studied physics and mathematics. She lost her first job as a school teacher, when she refused to join an examination board which applied special conditions for Jewish candidates. She is married to the human-rights activist Igor Gerashchenko. They have constantly protested against the violation of human rights and they were first arrested when demonstrating in Pushkin Square about the fate of Andrei Sakharov. She was ordered to 'stop writing poetry', which naturally she disregarded. In 1983 she was sentenced to seven years' hard labour. Her book of poems about life in prison, *No, I'm Not Afraid*, was translated by David McDuff and published in 1986.

Margaret Reckord is a Jamaican poet and editor of the visual arts magazine *Arts Jamaica*. The three poems included here are from her collection, *Upmountain*.

Michèle Roberts was born in 1949, educated at a convent and then went to Oxford University. She joined various women's writers' collectives which produced several anthologies: *Cutlasses and Earrings* (1976), *Licking the Bed Clean* (1978), *Tales I Tell My Mother*, short stories (1978), *Smile Smile Smile Smile* (1980). She also contributed to *One Foot on the Mountain* (1979), and has written three novels.

Magaly Sánchez was born in Holguin, Cuba, in 1940. She was a student when the revolutionary movement gained momentum and was active in producing a clandestine newspaper, where her first writings were published. 'I came to poetry early, spontaneously, in an almost confessional act . . . the revolution taught us that a poem can have the force of a cannon shot and the tenderness of a child and can bear the greatest beauty.' She also writes short stories, for children and for many papers and magazines.

Sappho was born on the island of Lesbos in the seventh century BC. She married and had a daughter, Kleis. One of the finest lesbian poets, she has always caused much controversy by her writing. Plato called her the tenth muse and a medieval pope – Gregory VIII – thought her so subversive that he ordered her poems to be burnt. Luckily much of it survived in fragments and quotations.

Penelope Shuttle was born in 1947 and now lives in Cornwall with her husband, Peter Redgrove, and young daughter. She began writing in her early teens, publishing poems in numerous magazines. She has written five novels, two radio plays and several collections of poetry, including *The Orchard Upstairs* (1980), *The Child-Stealer* (1983), and *The Lion from Rio* (1986). She has collaborated with Peter Redgrove on several books; their major work was *The Wise Wound*, a psychological study of the menstrual cycle. She has won many awards and gives frequent broadcasts and public readings of her poetry.

Mary Lonnberg Smith went to Cornell University for two years and graduated at UC Berkeley, having majored in English, and then worked as a social worker in Hayward, California. She lived with her husband Leonard Smith and son, Benjamin, in Santa Cruz until her tragic death in a car accident. She was deeply interested in meditation and yoga and played the cello as a hobby.

Noémia da Sousa was born in Mozambique in 1927. As a journalist she was associated with the militant African literature in Portuguese. She continually wrote and protested against the repressive Portuguese government and was eventually forced into exile in France where she continued to write under the pseudonym Vera Micaia.

Eunice de Souza lives and works in Bombay. Some of her poems are to be published in a collection, *Women and Dutch Painting* (1987–8). Her first collection, *Fix*, was published in Bombay in 1979; other poems have appeared in *Making for the Open*, edited by Carol Rumens.

Genevieve Taggard (1894–1948) spent much of her childhood in Hawaii, where her father was a fruit farmer, her mother a teacher. Later she attended the University of California in Berkeley. A feminist and socialist, much of her work appeared in *The Liberator*. Her publications include *Collected Poems: 1918–1938, Long View* (1942), *Slow Music* (1946) and a biography, *The Life and Times of Emily Dickinson* (1930).

Éva Tóth was born in Debrecen, Hungary, in 1943. She is a poet, translator and editor, now living in Budapest. Her publications include two books of verse, translations from Spanish, Italian and French, and several children's books. Her latest work is an anthology of Hungarian poetry from earliest times to the present, translated into Spanish.

Sojourner Truth (1797–1883) was born into slavery and known as Isabella but she was later freed by the New York Emancipation Act 1827. She left the state in 1843 with a bag of clothes and 25 cents and adopted the name that would become famous. She travelled the East Coast performing for white audiences, who were fascinated by her size – she was unusually tall – and by her wit and singing. A great performer, in 1850 she launched an assault on white people's apathy towards the slavery issue. At the end of the Civil War, she was appointed head councillor at Freedman's village in Virginia. Realising that the recently released slaves were denied respect and a decent life style, she spent the last years of her life campaigning and lecturing for land ownership for former slaves and spent years collecting signatures for a petition to be presented to Congress. She died in 1883, disillusioned with America's disregard for truth and human rights. The petition had been left on a shelf, unwanted and ignored. However, she left behind an extraordinary legacy of courage and endurance.

Yolanda Ulloa was born in Cuba in 1948. She graduated in dramatic arts and, in 1974, went to Hungary for a course in theatre. She is now an actress and works with the Bertold Brecht Political Theatre Group in Havana. She has published a book of poems called *The Songs of Benjamin*. She does voluntary work with children, is a member of the Cuban Communist Party, is married and has a daughter.

Julia Vinograd lives in Berkeley, California, where she is well known as a street poet. She has published two books of poetry, *Cannibal Crumbs* and *Street Scenes* (1987).

Alice Walker was born in 1944 in Eatonton, Georgia, the youngest of eight children. She began to write poetry while still a child and her collections now include *Once, Revolutionary Petunias, Good Night Willie Lee, I'll See You in the Morning* and *Horses Make a Landscape Look More Beautiful*. She has written three novels, including the Pulitzer Prize-winning *The Color Purple*. Always politically active, her involvement with the civil rights movement began when she was a student. She has a daughter and lives in San Francisco.

Susan Wallbank was born in London in 1943. She studied art, then went on to train as a counsellor. For the last eight years she has specialised in the field of bereavement. She is married and has three daughters. 'If I have any beliefs or commitments I suspect they emerge in my poetry.' Her poetry has been published in three anthologies: *Hard Feelings, Bread and Roses, All in the End is Harvest*. She gives readings of her poetry, which she enjoys immensely.

Michelene Wandor is a poet, playwright and critic. She was born in London in 1940. From 1971 to 1982 she was poetry editor of *Time Out*. Her work includes radio plays and features, and a dramatisation of Eugene Sue's The *Wandering Jew* (National Theatre, 1987); her publications include *Gardens of Eden* and *Upbeat* (poetry); *Guests in the Body* (stories); critical work on the theatre: *Carry On, Understudies* and *Look Back in Gender*. She is also the editor of an annual anthology of plays by women.

Anna Wickham (1884–1947) had the gift of crystallising her thoughts and experiences into poetry almost instantaneously. She wrote it down on whatever was to hand, odd scraps of paper, even the kitchen wall! Because of this her poetry has a rare immediacy and accessibility. In her life, which she lived to the full, she was pulled in many directions: woman as poet, mother, wife, daughter. The conflicts were deep and inspired much of her writing. She was married to a lawyer – Patrick Hepburn – and her greatest happiness was with her sons. She attracted people throughout her life and her friends were amongst the celebrities of the day. In her later years, a powerful influence was her relationship with Natalie Barney with whom she conducted a passionate correspondence. In 1947 she committed suicide. Her collections of poetry include *Songs of John Oland* (1911), *The Contemplative Quarry* (1915), *The Man with a Hammer* (1916), *The Little Old House* (1921), *Thirty-Six New Poems* (1936), *Selected Poems* (1972), and *The Writings of Anna Wickham* (Virago Press, 1984), which includes some autobiographical prose.

Sherley Anne Williams was born in 1944 in Bakersfield, California. She is now a member of the literature department at the University of California/San Diego. Her stories and poems have been published in the *Massachusetts Review, Ismael*, the *Pan Africanist, New Letters* and the *Iowa Review*. Publications include *Give Birth to Brightness, A Thematic Study in Neo-Black Literature* (1972) and *The Peacock Poems* (1977). 'Poetry is the most subjective means I have of making a metaphor of experience. Yet, no matter how personal that experience may seem, I am always aware that someone has been there before me . . . I like to hear the sound of words crashing against the space which surrounds them . . . I write, describe mental images which give rise to situation, emotion, idea. And abstractions are dealt with in an in-abstract, common manner – which, for me, is the level at which ideas are manifest in living.'

Mary Wilson, the wife of Sir Harold Wilson, was born at Diss, Norfolk, and is the daughter of a Congregational minister. She spent her childhood in East Anglia and has lived in various parts of the Lake District and Sussex, where she was at school. She began to write poetry at the age of six. Mary Wilson has two sons and twin granddaughters. She now lives part of the time in London, and the other part in the Isles of Scilly.

Daisy Yamora was born in Nicaragua, where she now works for the Ministry of Culture, which published her book *La Violenta Espuma* in 1981.

Yosano Akiko (1878–1942) was born in Japan. She studied with, and married, Yosano Hiroshi. Together they founded the New Poetry Society. Her poetry was quickly recognised and she wrote many collections, novels, children's stories, essays and fairy tales. She was a leading pacifist, feminist and socialist and found the time to have eleven children.